HR Best Practices Series

Leaves of Absence

in California

A closer look at your business and current California law

CALIFORNIA
CHAMBER of
COMMERCE℠

Helping California Business Do Business®

Published by
California Chamber of Commerce
P.O. Box 1736
Sacramento, CA 95812-1736

Copyright © 2005 by California Chamber of Commerce

All rights reserved. Not to be reproduced in any form without written permission from the publisher.

ISBN 1-57997-100-8

5 4 3 2 1

The information compiled in this handbook is being provided by the California Chamber of Commerce as a service to the business community. Although every effort has been made to ensure the accuracy and completeness of this information, the California Chamber of Commerce and the contributors and reviewers of this publication cannot be responsible for any errors and omissions, nor any agency's interpretations, applications and changes of regulations described herein.

This publication is designed to provide accurate and authoritative information in a highly summarized manner with regard to the subject matter covered. It is sold with the understanding that the publisher and others associated with this publication are not engaged in rendering legal, technical or other professional service. If legal and other expert assistance is required, the services of competent professionals should be sought.

This publication is available from:

California Chamber of Commerce
P.O. Box 1736
Sacramento, CA 95812-1736
(916) 444-6670
http://www.calchamberstore.com

Contents

What's New for 2005? vii

About This Product. xi
    Forms CD xi
    Structure. xi
    Formatting. xii
    Editors xiii
    California Chamber of Commerce Resources. xiii

Chapter 1
Getting Started 1
    Does This Law Apply to Me?. 1
    How Different Types of Leave Interact 3
    Guide to Absences and Payments 4
    California Domestic Partner Rights and Responsibilities Act 10
    COBRA and Cal-COBRA 12

Chapter 2
Pregnancy Disability Leave 15
    Pregnancy Disability Leave Defined. 16
    Handling Employee Requests. 20
    Controlling PDL. 23
    Paying the Employee 27

Contents

  Continuing Benefits.. 30
  Handling the Employee's Return to Work 32
  Forms and Checklists 35
  Further Information... 40

Chapter 3
Family Medical Leave...................................41
  Family Medical Leave Defined 43
  Handling Employee Requests 48
  Controlling Family Medical Leave..................................... 53
  Paying the Employee 60
  Continuing Benefits.. 62
  Handling the Employee's Return to Work 64
  Forms and Checklists 68
  Further Information... 70

Chapter 4
Disability Leave 71
  What is a Disability?... 72
  Who is a Qualified Individual?.. 73
  Disability Leave Defined 75
  Handling Employee Requests 76
  Controlling Disability Leave... 78
  Paying the Employee 79
  Continuing Benefits.. 80
  Handling the Employee's Return to Work 81
  Forms and Checklists 82
  Further Information... 82

Chapter 5
Workplace Injury and Illness. 83
Workplace Injury and Illness Defined 84
Handling Employee Requests. 88
Controlling Workers' Compensation. 92
Paying the Employee 93
Continuing Benefits 94
Handling the Employee's Return to Work 95
Forms and Checklists. 96
Further Information 99

Chapter 6
SDI and PFL. 101
State Disability Insurance Defined 102
SDI Qualifying Events 103
Medical Certification. 104
SDI Benefits 105
Paid Family Leave Defined 107
PFL Qualifying Events 109
PFL Benefits 110
Transfers, Benefits, and Reinstatement Rights 112
What You Should Do. 113
Further Information 114

Chapter 7
Sick Leave and Kin Care 115
Sick Leave/Kin Care Defined 115
Handling Employee Requests. 116
Controlling Sick Leave and Kin Care 117
Paying the Employee 117

Continuing Benefits..118
Handling the Employee's Return to Work............................119
Forms and Checklists.. 120

Chapter 8
Vacation and Paid Time Off.................................121
Vacation and PTO Defined... 121
Handling Employee Requests...................................... 122
Controlling Vacation and PTO..................................... 122
Paying the Employee 124
Continuing Benefits.. 125
Forms and Checklists... 126

Chapter 9
Other Legally Protected Absences...........................127
Military Service Leave 127
Jury/Witness Duty Leave.. 132
Domestic Violence/Sexual Assault Victims Leave 134
Victims of Crime Leave 138
Reasonable Accommodation for Rehabilitation......................141
Volunteer Civil Service Personnel Leave 143
School Appearance Leave 145
School Activities Leave... 146
Voting Leave... 148
Employee Literacy Assistance..................................... 149
Forms and Checklists...151

Chapter 10

Other Optional Leaves 155

    Holidays and Personal Holidays 155

    Floating Holidays 158

    Bereavement Leave 160

    Unpaid Personal Leave 162

    Unpaid Sick Leave 164

    Sabbaticals 165

    Education Leave 166

    Forms and Checklists 167

Index 169

What's New for 2005?

This preface shows the additions and changes for this edition of **Leaves of Absence in California**. These changes are detailed in chapter order.

Getting Started

- "Does This Law Apply to Me?" has been updated to standardize legal topic references across all Chamber products. See Table 3 on page 2.

- "How Different Types of Leave Interact" has been updated to include information on family medical leave rights for registered domestic partners. See Table 4 on page 3.

- "Guide to Absences and Payments" has been updated to include information on CFRA leave to care for a registered domestic partner. See Table 5 on page 5.

- A new section has been added describing the California Domestic Partner Rights and Responsibilities Act of 2003 that became effective January 1, 2005. Along with other provisions, this legislation extends state family medical leave rights (CFRA) to registered domestic partners, affecting how family medical leave benefits are provided. See "California Domestic Partner Rights and Responsibilities Act" on page 10.

- A new section has been added providing basic information on COBRA and Cal-COBRA. See "COBRA and Cal-COBRA" on page 12.

- COBRA forms have been renamed and updated to comply with new federal COBRA regulations. See Table 6 on page 12.

    - The *COBRA Election Form (California)* is now called *COBRA Continuation Coverage Election Notice (California Employees)*; and

    - The *COBRA Election Form (Outside California)* is now called *COBRA Continuation Coverage Election Notice (Outside California)*.

- The following forms have been added to the CD included with this product. See Table 6 on page 12.
  - *Acknowledgement of Receipt of Notification of COBRA Rights*; and
  - *COBRA - Notice to Plan Administrator.*

Pregnancy Disability Leave

A new "Forms and Checklists" table lists PDL forms and summarizes how to use them. See Table 8 on page 35.

Family Medical Leave

- Recent legislation extends state family medical leave rights (CFRA) to registered domestic partners, affecting how family medical leave benefits are provided. See:
  - "Reasons for leave" in Table 9 on page 42;
  - "Serious Health Conditions and Family Care" on page 44;
  - "Obtaining Medical Certification" on page 50; and
  - "Domestic Partners and CFRA" on page 56.
- A new "Forms and Checklists" table lists family medical leave forms and summarizes how to use them. See Table 10 on page 68.
- The *Federal Family and Medical Leave Act Poster (Spanish)* form has been added to the CD included with this product. See Table 10 on page 69.

Disability Leave

A new "Forms and Checklists" table lists disability leave forms and summarizes how to use them. See Table 13 on page 82.

Workplace Injury and Illness

- As of January 1, 2005, if you offer a medical provider network (MPN), you retain control of an injured employee's medical care indefinitely. See "What You Should Do" on page 89.

- A new "Forms and Checklists" table lists workers' compensation forms and summarizes how to use them. See Table 16 on page 96.

- The following forms have been added to the CD included with this product. See Table 16 on page 96.

    - *Guidelines for Determining OSHA Log 300 Recordability;*

    - *Optional Worksheet to Help You Fill Out the Annual Summary (Form 300A);* and

    - *Summary of Work-Related Injuries and Illnesses (Form 300A).*

SDI and PFL

- Recent legislation has changed the concurrency relationship of FMLA/CFRA leave for leave taken to care for a registered domestic partner. See "Relationship to current leave laws" in Table 19 on page 108.

- The maximum weekly PFL benefit increased from $728 to $840.

Sick Leave and Kin Care

A new "Forms and Checklists" table lists sick leave/kin care forms and summarizes how to use them. See Table 21 on page 120.

Vacation and Paid Time Off

A new "Forms and Checklists" table lists vacation/PTO forms and summarizes how to use them. See Table 22 on page 126.

Other Legally Protected Absences

- A new federal law affects rights and benefits for veterans and employees who are called for military duty, extending the period for continuation of health care coverage and establishing a new posting requirement for employers. See:

    - "The Law Explained" on page 127;

    - "Continuing Benefits" on page 129; and

    - Step 2 in "What You Should Do" on page 131.

- The following forms have been added to the CD included with this product. See Table 23 on page 151.
    - *Domestic Violence/Sexual Assault Victims Leave Policy (1-24 Employees)*; and
    - *Domestic Violence/Sexual Assault Victims Leave Policy (25 or More Employees)*.
- A new "Forms and Checklists" table lists protected absences forms and summarizes how to use them. See Table 23 on page 151.

Other Optional Leaves

A new "Forms and Checklists" table lists optional leaves forms and summarizes how to use them. See Table 24 on page 167.

About This Product

This product is designed to help California employers effectively manage the many types of leaves of absence that they must or may provide to employees.

Forms CD

Throughout this book, you'll find references to forms, sample policies, and checklists to help you manage leaves and comply with leave laws. Most of these are included on the Forms CD that comes with this book. Others are available from the California Chamber of Commerce or government agencies.

Structure

Chapter 1, "Getting Started," provides basic information to introduce you to types of leave, leave laws, and other laws that affect how you manage leaves of absence.

The remaining chapters are organized according to major leaves of absence categories, such as Chapter 2, "Pregnancy Disability Leave"; Chapter 3, "Family Medical Leave"; Chapter 7, "Sick Leave and Kin Care"; and so on.

Each chapter is divided into the functional areas you are likely to encounter as you manage the process. Thus, Chapter 2, "Pregnancy Disability Leave," establishes the same basic pattern for the rest of the book:

Table 1. Sections Within Each Chapter

Section	Description
Pregnancy Disability Leave Defined	Gives a broad overview of the law and defines the major terms and concepts you will need to understand.
Handling Employee Requests	Covers the applicable law and what to do should an employee inform you of the need to take time off because of her pregnancy.

Table 1. Sections Within Each Chapter *(continued)*

Section	Description
Controlling PDL	Provides information about what types of leave may interact with PDL, and how (where possible) to manage the amount of time the employee is off work.
Paying the Employee	Covers wage replacement issues, if any, and how to apply them.
Continuing Benefits	Details how employee benefits are handled during the leave.
Handling the Employee's Return to Work	Covers the transition from the leave of absence to the employee's restarting work.
Forms and Checklists	Provides brief descriptions of the most important forms associated with the process. 💡 You can find these forms on the CD included with this product.
Further Information	References additional resources outside this product.

Within task-based sections, content is organized into intuitive "The Law Explained" and "What You Should Do" subsections, which provide descriptions of various laws and tasks followed by the steps you should take to comply.

Formatting

This product uses formatting conventions to help you identify information.

Table 2. Formatting

Italics	Identifies emphasized text and form and checklist names.
Bold Italics	Identifies Chamber products and website addresses.
New for 2005	Identifies information that has been added or changed in this product since last year's edition. These changes are summarized in "What's New for 2005?" on page vii.
❗	Identifies information to which you should pay close attention.
💡	Identifies definitions of terms, as well as helpful advice.

Editors

Susan Kemp is Senior Labor Law Counsel and a Helpline Consultant for the California Chamber of Commerce. Susan has written and edited several Chamber publications on topics such as employee handbooks, sexual harassment investigations, family and medical leave, and exempt/non-exempt employees.

She graduated from South Texas College of Law and the University of Houston, and has been admitted to the bar in both California and Texas. Her previous experience includes human resources and training for a Fortune 500 company and litigation for an insurance defense firm.

California Chamber of Commerce Resources

The California Chamber of Commerce produces software and publications to help employers comply with employment laws and California Occupational Safety and Health (Cal/OSHA) regulations. For more information on California Chamber products, visit **http://www.calchamberstore.com**.

- **HRCalifornia.com**

    A comprehensive website designed to help California human resource (HR) managers deal with issues that come up every day. It's easy to navigate, great for powerful searches, and contains dozens of user-friendly, time-saving HR features. Visit the site at **http://www.hrcalifornia.com**.

- **2005 California Labor Law Digest**
- **2005 California Human Resource Essentials**
- **HR Best Practices Series**:
    - *Workers' Compensation in California*
    - *Sexual Harassment in California*
    - *Recruiting, Performance & Termination in California*
- **Writing Your California Employee Handbook 2005** software
- **Required Notices Kit** (includes the **Employer Poster**)
- **Labor Law Extra**

    A free e-mail service designed to give you employment law updates as they happen. Register at **http://www.laborlawextra.com**.

- **Wage Order Wizard**

    A free online tool designed to help you determine which Industrial Welfare Commission (IWC) Wage Order(s) your company must post, located at ***http://www.hrcalifornia.com/wageorders***.

- **Poster Update Website**

    A free service where you can get up-to-date information about required postings, including Wage Orders, located at ***http://www.hrcalifornia.com/poster***.

Chapter 1
Getting Started

Managing leaves of absence for your California employees can be a complicated process. Several factors are at play — some are mandated by law and others you control by virtue of your written policy or actual practice. To a large extent, your policies determine the time off your employees may take. However, there are numerous state and federal laws you must follow as well.

Legal mandates generally come in two forms: those which dictate time off that you must provide (such as pregnancy disability leave or time off for voting) and those that provide compensation for certain absences (such as paid family leave or state disability insurance). Still others, such as workers' compensation, are both mandated leaves of absence *and* paid benefits during the time off.

Does This Law Apply to Me?

The number of employees you have is a key factor in determining which laws apply to your company: 50 or more employees marks the beginning of federal Family and Medical Leave Act (FMLA) leave and state California Family Rights Act (CFRA) leave. Other laws, such as for jury duty and victims of crime leave, apply to all companies, regardless of size. The following table helps you determine which laws apply to you according to the number of employees you have.

Table 3. Does This Law Apply to Me?

Law/requirement	All employers	4 or more	5 or more	15 or more	20 or more	25 or more	50 or more	75 or more
California Family Rights Act (CFRA)							✓	✓
Disability Leave			✓	✓		✓	✓	✓
Domestic Violence/Sexual Assault Victims Leave	✓							
Family and Medical Leave Act (FMLA)							✓	✓
Jury/Witness Duty Leave	✓							
Kin Care	✓							
Military Service Leave	✓							
Paid Family Leave (PFL)	✓							
Pregnancy Disability Leave (PDL)			✓	✓		✓	✓	✓
School Activities Leave						✓	✓	✓
School Appearance Leave	✓							
State Disability Insurance (SDI)	✓							
Victims of Crime Leave	✓							
Volunteer Civil Service Leave	✓							
Voting Leave	✓							
Workers' Compensation	✓							

How Different Types of Leave Interact

Your starting point for compliance is to determine how many employees your company has; but that is only the beginning. Another key factor in California is the fact that mandated or voluntary leaves of absence interact with each other, and can be taken either consecutively (as with CFRA leave, which begins only after PDL ends) or concurrently (as with PDL and FMLA leave, which can be used at the same time). In turn, how you draft and apply your own voluntary policies has a significant impact on the amount of leave your employees can take.

Whether the different leaves run consecutively or concurrently will have a significant impact on how you manage the time your employees are on leave. Table 4 helps illustrate the relationships among the various types of mandated and voluntary leave.

Once you review Table 3 and know which laws apply to you, review the following table to see how the key leaves of absence interact with each other.

Table 4. How Different Types of Leave Interact

This leave	Runs concurrently with	Under these conditions
PDL (See Chapter 2, "Pregnancy Disability Leave")	FMLA	Always, if you notify the employee.
	CFRA	Never.
	Workers' compensation	Never.
	Disability	If your disability policy says so (it should).
FMLA (See Chapter 3, "Family Medical Leave")	CFRA	For all leaves except pregnancy disability and you notify the employee. **New for 2005** Employees in a registered domestic partnership are not entitled to FMLA leave to care for their partner, but are entitled to CFRA leave for this purpose; see "Domestic Partners and CFRA" in Chapter 3, page 56.
	Workers' compensation	If there is a work-related injury or illness, the employee cannot work, and you notify the employee.
	Disability	If your disability policy says so (it should) and you notify the employee.
	PDL	If the employee is on leave due to pregnancy disability and you notify the employee.

Table 4. How Different Types of Leave Interact *(continued)*

This leave	Runs concurrently with	Under these conditions
CFRA (See Chapter 3, "Family Medical Leave")	FMLA	For all leaves except pregnancy disability and you notify the employee. **New for 2005** Employees in a registered domestic partnership are entitled to CFRA leave to care for their partner, but are not entitled to FMLA leave for this purpose; see "Domestic Partners and CFRA" in Chapter 3, page 56.
	Workers' compensation	If there is a work-related injury or illness, the employee cannot work, and you notify the employee.
	Disability	If your disability policy says so (it should) and you notify the employee.
	PDL	Never.
Workers' compensation (See Chapter 5, "Workplace Injury and Illness")	FMLA/CFRA	Always, if there is a work-related injury or illness, the employee cannot work, and you notify the employee.
	Disability	If your disability policy says so (it should) and you notify the employee.
	PDL	Never.
Disability (See Chapter 4, "Disability Leave")	FMLA/CFRA	If you are covered, your disability policy says so (it should), and you notify the employee.
	Workers' compensation	If your disability policy says so (it should) and you notify the employee.
	PDL	If your disability policy says so (it should) and you notify the employee.

Guide to Absences and Payments

Once you know whether a leave of absence law applies to you, and how it may interact with other mandated or voluntary leaves, you need to determine whether the employee on leave is entitled to pay for the time off. Once again, the pay may come in the form of a state- or federally-mandated benefit (such as disability insurance or paid family leave), or a payment you choose to offer (such as sick pay or vacation pay).

The following table shows the relationships between the various leaves of absence, and whether there are any required or discretionary wage replacements.

Table 5. Guide to Absences and Payments

If absence is for this	This law may apply	This type of payment may apply
Employee is disabled by pregnancy, and you have fewer than 50 employees or the employee is not eligible for FMLA/CFRA	PDL	SDI Sick pay Vacation Paid time off (PTO)
Employee is disabled by pregnancy, you have more than 50 employees, and the employee is eligible for FMLA/CFRA	FMLA running concurrently with PDL	SDI Sick pay Vacation PTO
To bond with a new child after birth or placement for adoption or foster care, you have more than 50 employees, and the employee is eligible for FMLA/CFRA	CFRA for baby bonding	PFL (for a claim beginning on or after July 1, 2004) Sick pay Vacation PTO See "Paying the Employee" in Chapter 2, page 27
Serious illness or injury of employee, you have more than 50 employees, the illness or injury is not work related, and the employee is eligible for FMLA/CFRA	FMLA/CFRA	SDI Sick pay Vacation PTO See "Paying the Employee" in Chapter 5, page 93
Serious illness or injury of employee's spouse, parent, or child; you have more than 50 employees; and the employee is eligible for FMLA/CFRA	FMLA /CFRA Kin care	PFL (for a claim beginning on or after July 1, 2004) Sick pay Vacation PTO

Table 5. Guide to Absences and Payments *(continued)*

If absence is for this	This law may apply	This type of payment may apply
New for 2005 Serious illness or injury of employee's registered domestic partner, you have more than 50 employees, and the employee is eligible for CFRA	CFRA Kin care	PFL (for a claim beginning on or after July 1, 2004) Sick pay/kin care Vacation PTO See "California Domestic Partner Rights and Responsibilities Act" on page 10, and "Domestic Partners and CFRA" in Chapter 3, page 56
Qualified disabled employee and disability is not work- or pregnancy-related	Leave as an accommodation for disability	SDI Sick pay Vacation PTO See "Paying the Employee" in Chapter 4, page 79
Work-related illness/injury	Workers' compensation FMLA/CFRA (if covered employer and eligible employee)	Workers' compensation Sick pay Vacation PTO See "Paying the Employee" in Chapter 5, page 93
Serious illness or injury of employee; you have fewer than 50 employees or the employee is not eligible for FMLA/CFRA; and the injury or illness is not work related	Your sick leave policy	SDI Sick Pay Vacation PTO See "Paying the Employee" in Chapter 7, page 117

Table 5. Guide to Absences and Payments *(continued)*

If absence is for this	This law may apply	This type of payment may apply
Serious illness/injury of employee's spouse, parent, child, domestic partner, or domestic partner's child, and you are an employer who offers sick pay	Your sick leave policy Kin care	PFL (for a claim beginning on or after July 1, 2004) Kin care See "Paying the Employee" in Chapter 7, page 117
Vacation	Your policy	Vacation PTO See "Paying the Employee" in Chapter 8, page 124
Military service/training	Uniformed Services Employment and Reemployment Rights Act (USERRA)	Depends on employee status (exempt or non-exempt) and length of time the employee is away Employees may use vacation or PTO, but you may not require it See "Military Service Leave" in Chapter 9, page 127
Jury/witness duty	Employees must serve if called and you cannot discriminate against the employee in any way for taking time off to serve on a jury or appear as a witness	Depends on employee status (exempt or non-exempt) and your policy Vacation PTO See "Jury/Witness Duty Leave" in Chapter 9, page 132
Domestic violence/sexual assault, and you have fewer than 25 employees	Time off to seek a temporary restraining order or other health/safety assistance	Depends on employee status (exempt or non-exempt) and your policy Vacation PTO See "Domestic Violence/Sexual Assault Victims Leave" in Chapter 9, page 134

Table 5. Guide to Absences and Payments *(continued)*

If absence is for this	This law may apply	This type of payment may apply
Domestic violence/sexual assault, and you have 25 or more employees	Up to 12 weeks to seek counseling, housing, and medical care	Depends on employee status (exempt or non-exempt) and your policy Vacation PTO See "Domestic Violence/Sexual Assault Victims Leave" in Chapter 9, page 134
Attendance at judicial proceedings related to a violent crime	Unlimited time off for eligible employees to attend judicial proceedings	Depends on employee status (exempt or non-exempt) Vacation PTO Sick pay See "Victims of Crime Leave" in Chapter 9, page 138
Emergency duty for volunteer civil service personnel	Volunteer civil service leave	Depends on employee status (exempt or non-exempt) and your policy See "Volunteer Civil Service Personnel Leave" in Chapter 9, page 143
Training for volunteer firefighter, and you have 50 or more employees	Maximum of 14 days per calendar year to engage in fire or law enforcement training	Depends on status of employee (exempt or non-exempt) and your policy See "Volunteer Civil Service Personnel Leave" in Chapter 9, page 143
Child suspended from school	Time off to appear on behalf of suspended child	Vacation PTO See "School Appearance Leave" in Chapter 9, page 145

Table 5. Guide to Absences and Payments (continued)

If absence is for this	This law may apply	This type of payment may apply
Participation in school activity, and you have 25 or more employees	School activity leave	Vacation PTO See "School Activities Leave" in Chapter 9, page 146
Drug/alcohol rehabilitation, and you have five or more employees	Reasonable accommodation for a disability	SDI Sick pay Vacation PTO See "Paying the Employee" in Chapter 4, page 79
Voting	Time off for voting	Up to two hours of paid leave See "Voting Leave" in Chapter 9, page 148
Literacy assistance	Reasonable accommodation should an employee request literacy assistance	Your policy governs whether you pay for this time off See "Employee Literacy Assistance" in Chapter 9, page 149
Holiday/floating holiday	No law specifies time off for holidays or floating holidays	Your policy governs whether you pay for this time off See "Holidays and Personal Holidays" in Chapter 10, page 155, and "Floating Holidays" in Chapter 10, page 158
Bereavement	No law specifies time off for bereavement	Your policy governs whether you pay for this time off See "Bereavement Leave" in Chapter 10, page 160
Unpaid personal leave Unpaid sick leave	No law specifies time off for unpaid personal leave or unpaid sick leave	Not applicable See "Unpaid Personal Leave" in Chapter 10, page 162, and "Unpaid Sick Leave" in Chapter 10, page 164

Table 5. Guide to Absences and Payments *(continued)*

If absence is for this	This law may apply	This type of payment may apply
Sabbatical	No law specifies time off for sabbaticals	Your policy governs whether you will allow employees to take sabbaticals See "Sabbaticals" in Chapter 10, page 165
Education leave	No law specifies time off for education leave	Your policy governs whether you will allow employees to take education leave See "Education Leave" in Chapter 10, page 166

California Domestic Partner Rights and Responsibilities Act

New for 2005 The California Domestic Partner Rights and Responsibilities Act of 2003[1] became effective January 1, 2005. The Act:

- Gives domestic partners the same rights, protections, and benefits as are granted to, and imposed upon, spouses;

- Subjects domestic partners to the same responsibilities, obligations, and duties under law, whether they derive from statutes, administrative regulations, court rules, government policies, common law, or any other provisions or sources of law, as are granted to and imposed upon spouses;

- Grants registered domestic partners, with respect to a child of either of them, the same rights and obligations as those of a child of a spouse; and

- Gives domestic partners the same rights for leave under CFRA as that given to spouses and their children.

For more information, see "Domestic Partners and CFRA" in Chapter 3, page 56.

Definition of Domestic Partners

Domestic partners are two adults who have chosen to share one another's lives in an intimate and committed relationship of mutual caring.

---

1. Enacted as AB 205 in 2003

A domestic partnership is established in California when *all* of the following requirements are met:

- Both persons share the same residence. It is not necessary that the legal right to possess the common residence be in both of their names. Two people have a common residence even if one or both have additional residences. Domestic partners do not cease to have a common residence if one leaves the common residence but intends to return;

- Both persons agree to be jointly responsible for each other's basic living expenses incurred during the domestic partnership:

    - "Joint responsibility" means that each partner agrees to provide for the other partner's basic living expenses if the partner is unable to provide for herself or himself. Persons to whom these expenses are owed may enforce this responsibility if, in extending credit or providing goods or services, they relied on the existence of the domestic partnership and the agreement of both partners to be jointly responsible for those specific expenses; and

    - "Basic living expenses" means shelter, utilities, and all other costs directly related to the maintenance of the common household of the common residence of the domestic partners. It also means any other cost, such as medical care, if some or all of the cost is paid as a benefit because a person is another person's domestic partner;

- Neither person is married or a member of another domestic partnership;

- The two persons are not related by blood in a way that would prevent them from being married to each other in this state;

- Both persons are at least 18 years of age;

- When either of the following is true:

    - Both persons are members of the same sex; or

    - One or both persons meet the eligibility criteria under Title II of the Social Security Act as defined in 42 U.S.C. Section 402(a) for old-age insurance benefits or Title XVI of the Social Security Act as defined in 42 U.S.C. Section 1381 for aged individuals. Notwithstanding any other provision of this section, persons of opposite sexes may not constitute a domestic partnership unless one or both of the persons are over the age of 62.

- Both persons are capable of consenting to the domestic partnership;

- Neither person has previously filed a Declaration of Domestic Partnership with the Secretary of State that has not been terminated under Section 299; and

- Both file a Declaration of Domestic Partnership with the Secretary of State.

You may require documentation of an employee's domestic partnership relationship as recognized under state law. For more information about the domestic partnership registry, visit ***http://www.ss.ca.gov/dpregistry***.

COBRA and Cal-COBRA

New for 2005 The Consolidated Omnibus Budget Reconciliation Act of 1985 (COBRA) requires employers with 20 or more employees to offer all employees covered by health care the option of continuing to be covered by the company health plan at the worker's own expense for a period (usually 18 months) after employment ends.

Employees covered by COBRA have an additional 18 months of coverage under Cal-COBRA. California law provides for Cal-COBRA coverage (employers with 2–19 employees) for up to a total of 36 months.

The following table describes forms associated with COBRA and Cal-COBRA.

 You can find these forms on the CD included with this product.

Table 6. COBRA/Cal-COBRA Forms

Form name	What do I use it for?	When do I use it?	Who fills it out?	Where does it go?
Acknowledgement of Receipt of Notification of COBRA Rights **New for 2005**	To document that you have notified the employee of his/her COBRA rights. Required for *all* types of separation if your insurance plan has 20 or more participants.	Within 14 days of the time you are notified of a qualifying event.	Employee signs.	Send via certified mail to the employee and spouse.
Cal-COBRA - Notice to Carrier	To notify your insurance carrier that a Cal-COBRA qualifying event has occurred. Required for *all* types of separation if your insurance plan has 2–19 participants.	Within 30 days of the qualifying event of either separation or reduction in hours.	You do.	Send the original form to your insurance carrier within 30 days of the qualifying event. Keep a copy in your personnel records.

Table 6. COBRA/Cal-COBRA Forms

Form name	What do I use it for?	When do I use it?	Who fills it out?	Where does it go?
Cal-COBRA - Notice to Employee	To inform former employees about changes in group health plans. Required if you are changing health plans and have former employees protected by Cal-COBRA.	At least 30 days before a change in group plans.	You do.	Send the original form to each individual who has elected Cal-COBRA, along with information about the new group benefit plan(s), premiums, enrollment forms, instructions, and anything else necessary to allow the individual to continue coverage. Keep a copy in the employee's personnel record.
COBRA Continuation Coverage Election Notice (California Employees) **New for 2005**	To enable a California employee to elect COBRA coverage. Required for *all* types of separation if you: • Have 20 or more employees; • Provide an employee health plan; and • Self-administer COBRA.	Within 44 days of a qualifying event.	Employee.	Send via certified mail to the California employee and spouse.

Table 6. COBRA/Cal-COBRA Forms

Form name	What do I use it for?	When do I use it?	Who fills it out?	Where does it go?
COBRA Continuation Coverage Election Notice (Outside California) **New for 2005**	To enable an employee outside California to elect COBRA coverage. Required for *all* types of separation if you: • Have 20 or more employees, some of whom are outside California; • Provide an employee health plan; and • Self-administer COBRA.	Within 44 days of a qualifying event.	Employee.	Send via certified mail to the employee and spouse outside California.
COBRA - Notice to Plan Administrator **New for 2005**	To notify your COBRA administrator that a qualifying event has occurred. Required if you: • Have 20 or more employees; • Provide an employee health plan; and • Outsource COBRA administration.	Within 30 days of a qualifying event.	You do.	Send to the plan administrator.

Chapter 2

Pregnancy Disability Leave

This chapter explains the basic provisions and implications of pregnancy disability leave (PDL). It also provides you with task-based steps to follow when an employee requests PDL.

 The forms mentioned in this chapter are on the CD included with this product.

The following table provides a broad overview of PDL.

Table 7. Pregnancy Disability Leave

PDL issue	Requirement
Covered employers	PDL is state law, and applies to you if you employ five or more individuals. See "Who's Covered?" on page 17.
Maximum amount of leave	PDL provides a maximum of 4 months of leave, which translates to 17 weeks plus 3 days, or a total of 88 working days. It can run concurrently with federal Family and Medical Leave Act (FMLA) leave, but never with state California Family Rights Act (CFRA) leave. See "Controlling PDL" on page 23.
Employee eligibility	Employees who work for covered employers are eligible for PDL upon hire. See "Who's Covered?" on page 17.
Reasons for leave	Employees may use PDL if disabled by pregnancy, childbirth, or related medical condition. See "What's a Qualifying Event?" on page 17.
Employer responsibilities	When you learn that an employee is pregnant, you should send a notice to the employee, designating any time off related to the pregnancy as PDL. See "Required Posters and Notices" on page 18.
Interaction with other leaves	See "Controlling PDL" on page 23.

Table 7. Pregnancy Disability Leave *(continued)*

PDL issue	Requirement
Ending the employment relationship before the leave expires	The employee has no greater rights than if she were not pregnant. The right to reinstatement ends if the employment relationship ends. Employees on PDL are protected, however, from any adverse employment action for taking PDL. Seek legal counsel before terminating anyone on PDL. See "Handling the Employee's Return to Work" on page 32.

The following checklists, described in Table 8 on page 35, can help you audit your PDL-related compliance activities, with reminders of key milestones in the process. Have copies nearby as you work through this chapter, noting completed activities and steps you have yet to take or develop.

- *PDL Checklist for Employer Compliance (5–49 Employees)*;
- *PDL Documentation - For Employer Use Only (5–49 Employees)*;
- *PDL/FMLA Checklist for Employer Compliance (50 or More Employees)*; and
- *PDL/FMLA Documentation - For Employer Use Only (50 or More Employees)*.

Pregnancy Disability Leave Defined

PDL provides up to four months of leave for an employee who is disabled by pregnancy, childbirth, or a related medical condition. The disability period includes doctor-ordered bed rest and recovery from childbirth.

There is no waiting period or length of service requirement for employee eligibility. The pregnant employee's health care provider determines the length of the disability period. The leave need not be taken all at once — the pregnant employee may take PDL intermittently, as in the case of morning sickness early in the pregnancy, followed months later by the birth of the child. When the employee's disability ends, the pregnancy disability leave ends.

> If you have already established a policy that permits longer leaves for other types of disabilities, you must offer the same for pregnancy disability.

Who's Covered?

PDL is California law, and applies if you employ more than five people. The following entities are also covered, regardless of their number of employees:

- The state of California;
- All counties within the state of California;
- All cities within the state of California; and
- All other divisions and subdivisions of the state and its cities and counties.

Even if you employ fewer than five employees, you should consult legal counsel before terminating a pregnant employee. You may be found in violation of public policy, even if you are not technically covered by the law. California courts are increasingly holding small employers responsible for violations of "public policy," meaning that small employers may be as responsible as large ones for following the law.

The state sets public policy, utilizing its police power in order to protect the welfare, health, and peace of the people of California. When an aggrieved employee files a lawsuit or pursues a claim with a state agency, he/she alleges that the business did not live up to its responsibilities under what the state thinks it ought to as an employer. This type of claim must involve a state policy that:

- Is expressly set forth in either constitutional or statutory provisions;
- Is for the benefit of the public;
- Is substantial and fundamental; and
- Was well-established at the time of the employee's discharge.

What's a Qualifying Event?

In general terms, a qualifying event is an occurrence that makes an employee eligible for leave or other entitlements. A woman is considered disabled by pregnancy if, in the opinion of her health care provider, she is:

- Unable to work;
- Unable to perform any one of her essential duties;
- Unable to perform these functions without undue risk to herself;
- Suffering from severe morning sickness; or
- In need of prenatal care.

Chapter 2: Pregnancy Disability Leave

> Pregnancy in itself is not a qualifying event. In order to qualify for PDL, the employee must be able to prove that she is actually disabled by pregnancy.

Required Posters and Notices

The law requires you to display certain posters regarding employee pregnancy disability rights.[2] The required poster(s) depends upon how many employees your company has.

- Employers of 5–49 employees must post the *Pregnancy Disability Leave Poster* from the California Department of Fair Employment and Housing (DFEH); or
- Employers of 50 or more employees must display two posters:
    - *California Family Rights Act and Pregnancy Disability Poster* from the California DFEH; and
    - *Federal Family and Medical Leave Act Poster* from the federal Department of Labor (DOL).

If you have Spanish-speaking employees, you may need to display posters in both English and Spanish. For more information on these posters, see Table 8 on page 35 and Table 10 on page 68.

All posters must be displayed in a conspicuous place that is frequented by your employees (such as a break room or cafeteria).

The California Chamber of Commerce produces an all-in-one **Employer Poster** that contains all the required employer postings, in both English and Spanish, including the DFEH and DOL pregnancy disability notices. For more information, call (800) 331-8877 or visit our online store at ***http://www.calchamberstore.com***.

Employers Covered by PDL Only

If you employ 49 or fewer employees, or your employee does not meet the eligibility requirements for FMLA or CFRA, you must give the pregnant employee notice that she is eligible only for PDL. For more information, see "Who's Eligible?" in Chapter 3, page 43.

If you are covered by PDL only, you must provide your employee with:

- *Pregnancy Disability Leave Poster* as soon as you learn of the pregnancy. You must also provide this notice if an employee inquires about PDL or a transfer; and

---

2. 2 CCR Division 4, 7291.16 (a)

- Notice that the employee is entitled to PDL only. You can use the sample *Employee Letter - PDL Only*, described in Table 8 on page 37, to provide the notice. Send a copy to the employee at the beginning of the leave and keep a copy in the employee's confidential medical file, separate from her personnel file.

Employers Covered by PDL and FMLA/CFRA

If you employed 50 or more employees in 20 or more weeks in the current or preceding calendar year, and the pregnant employee is eligible for FMLA (see "Who's Eligible?" in Chapter 3, page 43), PDL runs concurrently with FMLA.

If you are covered by FMLA/CFRA, you must provide your eligible employee with:

- *California Family Rights Act and Pregnancy Disability Poster* as soon as you learn of the pregnancy. You must also provide this notice if an employee inquires about PDL or a transfer; and

- Notice that she is eligible for both PDL and FMLA at the time she informs you of her need for leave. You can use the *Employee Letter - PDL/FMLA* and *Employee Letter - CFRA Leave Taken after FMLA/PDL*, described in Table 8 on page 37, to provide the notice. Send a copy to the employee at the beginning of the leave and keep a copy in the employee's confidential medical file, separate from her personnel file.

What You Should Do

1. Develop a written PDL policy and include it in your employee handbook (if you have one). For appropriate language, see the sample *Pregnancy Disability Leave Policy (5 or More Employees)*, described in Table 8 on page 39.

2. If you have 50 or more employees, also develop written FMLA/CFRA policies and include them in your employee handbook (if you have one). For appropriate language, see the sample *Coordination of PDL with Family/Medical Leave Policy (50 or More Employees)*, described in Table 8 on page 37, and *Family/Medical Leave Policy (50 or More Employees)*, described in Table 10 on page 68.

 You can find these forms on the CD included with this product.

Handling Employee Requests

An employee walks into your office, informs you of her pregnancy, and says that she needs time off or a transfer. What do you do?

The Law Explained

The employee must provide you with at least verbal notice of her intent to use PDL and the approximate anticipated date the leave will begin. However, you cannot deny a request for PDL or transfer on the basis that the employee did not provide advance notice. Additionally, you cannot deny PDL, or replace the employee who takes PDL, because of business necessity or undue hardship. There are no exceptions to an employee's right to PDL.

Obtaining Medical Certification

You may require medical certification to verify an employee's pregnancy disability, or the employee's fitness to return to work, only if you require such certification for other types of temporary disability. If you do require medical certification, it must come from the employee's own doctor or other health care provider.

If an employee provides you with a physician's certification stating that she cannot work due to pregnancy, you must allow her to take PDL.

 Certification means written documentation from the employee's health care provider that the employee is disabled because of pregnancy, or that it is medically advisable for the employee to transfer to a less strenuous or hazardous position.

The medical certification for leave must contain:

- The date your employee became disabled by pregnancy;
- The probable duration of the disability; and
- A statement explaining that the employee is unable to work in her current job without undue risk to:
  - Herself;
  - Her unborn child; or
  - Other persons (coworkers, etc.).

You can use the *Certification of Physician or Practitioner for PDL or PDL/FMLA*, described in Table 8 on page 36, to obtain certification that the employee is disabled due to pregnancy. Keep the form in the employee's confidential medical file, separate from her personnel file.

Employees who are disabled by pregnancy will usually apply for state disability insurance (SDI) benefits. For the purpose of SDI benefits, the usual disability period for a normal pregnancy is up to four weeks before the expected delivery date, and up to six weeks after the delivery date. The doctor may certify a longer period of disability if the delivery is by cesarean section, if there are medical complications, or if the employee is unable to perform her regular or customary job duties.

Medical certification for a temporary transfer must contain:

- The date the transfer became medically advisable;
- The probable duration of the transfer; and
- A statement explaining that the employee's transfer is medically advisable because of her pregnancy.

 You can use the *Certification of Physician or Practitioner for Transfer Due to Pregnancy Disability*, described in Table 8 on page 36, to obtain certification of the need for the transfer. Keep the form in the employee's confidential medical file, separate from her personnel file.

Transfer to Alternative Position

The pregnant employee's health care provider may certify that the employee is unable to perform her current job, but could perform other duties. In cases where a transfer is medically advisable, and you can reasonably accommodate the transfer, you are required to do so.

You are not required to:

- Create additional employment;
- Discharge another employee;
- Violate the terms of a collective bargaining agreement;
- Transfer another employee with more seniority; or
- Promote or transfer an employee who is not qualified to perform the new job.

The employee who receives a medically advisable transfer is entitled to the compensation and benefits associated with the new position (regardless of whether they are more or less than before the transfer).

The pregnant employee may need to take PDL on an intermittent basis or work a reduced work schedule because of the pregnancy or planned medical treatment. In such cases, you may require that the employee transfer temporarily to an available alternative position. The alternative position must:

- Better accommodate the employee's need for leave than does her regular job;
- Have the same pay and benefits; and
- Be a position for which the employee is qualified.

The alternative position does not have to have equivalent duties.

 You can use the *Certification of Physician or Practitioner for Transfer Due to Pregnancy Disability*, described in Table 8 on page 35, to obtain certification of the need for the transfer. Keep the form in the employee's confidential medical file, separate from her personnel file.

Document your transfer policy in your employee handbook or other written policy. For appropriate language, see the sample *Temporary Transfers Policy*, described in Table 8 on page 40.

What You Should Do

When an employee requests leave for a pregnancy-related disability, you should:

1. Provide her with either the *Pregnancy Disability Leave Poster* or the *California Family Rights Act and Pregnancy Disability Poster*, if she is qualified for the leave.

2. Provide her with the required pamphlets including:

- *State Disability Insurance Provisions (DE 2515)*;
- *Paid Family Leave (DE 2511)*; and
- *For Your Benefit, California's Program for the Unemployed (Form 2320)*.

3. Request medical certification if she has not provided it, including:

- *Certification of Physician or Practitioner for PDL or PDL/FMLA*; and
- *Certification of Physician or Practitioner for Transfer Due to Pregnancy Disability*.

4. Send the employee the appropriate letter advising her that she will be placed on PDL or PDL/FMLA:

- *Employee Letter - PDL Only*;
- *Employee Letter - PDL/FMLA*; and
- *Employee Letter - CFRA Leave Taken after FMLA/PDL*.

5. Fill out a *Notice to Employee as to Change in Relationship*, documenting the employee's leave of absence at the time the leave begins.

6. Keep a copy of all documents in the employee's confidential medical file, separate from her personnel file. Use the *PDL Documentation - For Employer Use Only (5–49 Employees)* or *PDL/FMLA Documentation - For Employer Use Only (50 or More Employees)*, described in Table 8 on page 39, to manage the notification process, including the dates you provide and receive the documents.

 You can find most of these forms on the CD included with this product.

Controlling PDL

The amount of leave available to the employee who is pregnant will depend on whether you are covered by FMLA/CFRA or PDL only. This, in turn, depends on how many employees your company has. If you have fewer than 50 employees, you are generally covered by PDL only. The information in this section can help you determine the amount of leave that your employees may be entitled to. If you have 50 or more employees, review this section and also see Chapter 3, "Family Medical Leave for additional information about employee eligibility.

The Law Explained

For purposes of PDL, an employee is entitled to a maximum of 4months (17 weeks plus 3 days or 88 working days) of PDL. This calculation is based on the traditional eight-hour day, five-day workweek.

If the employee works less than a full-time, or an alternate workweek, the 4 months or 88 working days is calculated on a proportional basis.

> ***Example:*** An employee who works half-time, or 20 hours a week, would be entitled to 44 eight-hour days or 88 four-hour days of PDL.

Employees on PDL may take leave consecutively or intermittently. They may also take leave on a reduced schedule. You may only count the actual amount of leave taken against the PDL entitlement.

Example: If the employee takes off half of a day (four hours) for medical appointments, you may not count more than four hours against the PDL entitlement.

Calculating Leave – Employers Covered by PDL Only

If you have fewer than 50 employees, or if you are covered by FMLA/CFRA but have an employee who is not eligible for it, the pregnant employee will only be entitled to the 88 working days (4 months) of leave for absences related to pregnancy, childbirth, or a related medical condition.

Example: A pregnant employee, early in her pregnancy, needs to use one-half day of leave every week for prenatal care. She does this for eight weeks, until she becomes fully disabled by the pregnancy and can no longer work without endangering the health of herself or her unborn child. Because she used a total of 4 days for prenatal care, and they count as PDL, she would have 84 days of PDL remaining.

It is also possible for an employee to take leave intermittently, as in the case of morning sickness early in the pregnancy.

Example: An employee takes PDL intermittently for severe morning sickness during the first few months of her pregnancy. She then returns to work on a full-time schedule until she takes PDL again: two weeks prior to the birth of her child and six weeks after delivery for recovery from childbirth. All of the pregnancy-related time off counts toward PDL.

Once the employee is no longer disabled by pregnancy, childbirth or a related medical condition, her PDL ends.

Example: An employee with a small advertising firm took eight weeks of PDL and has been released by her health care provider to return to work. She has been taking time off to care for the baby who is often ill, and she has exceeded her available sick time, including the time that would be available as "kin care." Can her employer terminate her?

As a small employer with less than 50 employees, the employer is not covered by FMLA/CFRA. The employer should advise the employee that she has exceeded the limit of her available sick pay. If the employee continues to take time off, the employer is free to take adverse action — up to, and including, termination.

Calculating Leave — Employers Covered by PDL, FMLA, and CFRA

If you employ 50 or more employees, you are generally covered by PDL, FMLA, and CFRA. Eligible employees who are absent for a reason related to the pregnancy should be placed on PDL running concurrently with FMLA. CFRA leave begins after the birth of the child, for purposes of baby bonding. It does not apply to the disability period itself. The following timeline shows the relationship between the maximum amount of PDL, running concurrently with FMLA, followed by the beginning of CFRA leave for baby bonding.

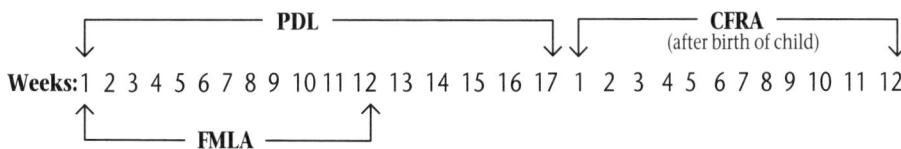

Usually, however, the pregnant employee will use only a portion of her PDL before her doctor releases her to return to work. In this case, the PDL running concurrently with FMLA (for the period of pregnancy disability) concludes, and the FMLA running concurrently with CFRA (for purposes of baby bonding) begins. In this case, the timeline (showing the maximum of 12 weeks for FMLA leave and for CFRA leave) is illustrated below:

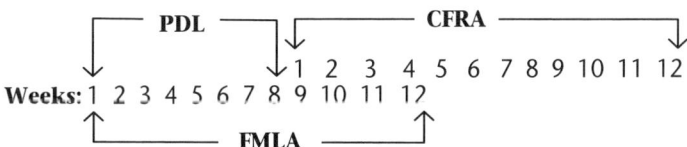

Example: A pregnant employee is disabled for two weeks prior to the birth of her child, and six weeks after. The total of eight weeks will be both PDL and FMLA, running concurrently. She then chooses to take time off to bond with the newborn child — CFRA leave. The first four weeks will be FMLA/CFRA, as she has not exhausted all of her FMLA leave (FMLA covers both pregnancy disability-related absences as well as time taken for baby bonding). The remaining eight weeks will be CFRA only.

Employee Still Disabled after Exhausting PDL/FMLA

There are, of course, situations when the employee's pregnancy disability extends past 88 working days. If she has not yet given birth to her child by the end of her PDL/FMLA or her disability continues beyond the 88 days, you are under no obligation to provide additional leave or job protection.

However, you must treat pregnancy disability the same as you treat other types of temporary disability.

> **Example:** If you gave six months of leave to an employee who suffered a heart attack, you must provide the same amount of leave to the employee disabled by pregnancy.

> **Example:** A pregnant employee is disabled for 100 days before the birth of her child. The first 12 weeks (60 working days) are PDL/FMLA, and the next 28 days are PDL only. She is not entitled to CFRA leave for baby bonding because she is still disabled by pregnancy and has not yet given birth. You may choose to allow her to take CFRA at this point, but you are not required to do so.

In this case, the timeline (showing the 100-day disability period) shows the gap between the end of the PDL and the beginning of CFRA leave for baby bonding. During this time period, the employee has no legal job protection.

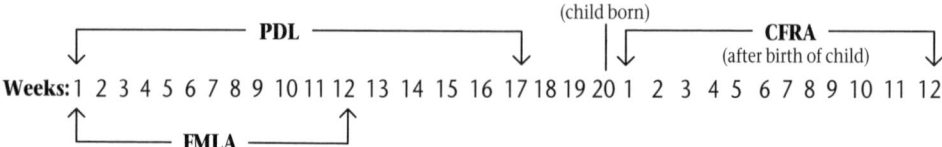

If, in the above example, the employee was disabled by pregnancy for 100 working days, and gave birth on the 101st day, she would be able to take CFRA leave beginning on day 101. Although the employee may continue to be disabled by childbirth, she has no PDL remaining. However, the child has been born, and she can now use CFRA leave for baby bonding.

Holidays

If a holiday occurs during the employee's leave, you may count the holiday as a day of PDL or PDL/FMLA leave. However, if your company ceases business for an entire week (for example, you shut down operations for the week of Christmas), you cannot count the week against the employee's PDL or PDL/FMLA leave.

What You Should Do

1. Send the employee the appropriate letter to put her on notice that any time off she takes for qualifying PDL reasons will count against her PDL or PDL/FMLA entitlement:

    - *Employee Letter - PDL Only*;

- *Employee Letter - PDL/FMLA*; or
- *Employee Letter - CFRA Leave Taken after FMLA/PDL.*

2. If you have provided other employees disability leave in excess of your PDL or PDL/FMLA obligations, be sure to give a disabled pregnant employee the same amount of leave (if needed).

3. Keep accurate records of the employee's PDL or PDL/FMLA-related absences.

4. If the employee exceeds the time allowed by the law, or by your policy, advise her immediately that her continued absence will result in losing her guaranteed job reinstatement or other employment rights and benefits, such as health insurance or seniority.

5. Keep any medical information that you receive in a separate, confidential file.

Paying the Employee

PDL is usually unpaid leave, although you may require that the employee use paid sick pay, or the employee may choose to use vacation or paid time off (PTO). These voluntary benefits are covered in see Chapter 7, "Sick Leave and Kin Care" and Chapter 8, "Vacation and Paid Time Off," but their relationships to the mandatory time off provisions of PDL, FML, and CFRA are covered here.

Eligible employees may also be entitled to disability insurance payments. These state-mandated benefits are covered in Chapter 6, "SDI and PFL," but their relationships to the mandatory time off provisions of PDL, FMLA, and CFRA are covered here as well.

The Law Explained

There is no legal requirement that you pay an employee on PDL. However, if you have a policy or practice of paying for other types of leave, and you have more than 15 employees, you must follow your more generous paid leave policy for an employee on PDL.

If you employ 5–14 employees, you do not have to pay an employee on PDL for more than six weeks of accrued paid leave, regardless of any paid leave policies you provide for other disabled employees.

You may allow or require an employee on PDL to use any accrued sick pay. However, you cannot require her to use accrued vacation or paid time off (PTO). You must allow the employee to use vacation or PTO if she would otherwise be eligible to do so.

Employees on PDL may also use disability insurance benefits for partial wage replacement while on leave.

The following shows a timeline of state disability insurance (SDI) and paid family leave (PFL) benefits during PDL, FMLA, and CFRA. The illustration shows the minimum 17 weeks for PDL and the maximum 12 weeks for FMLA and CFRA.

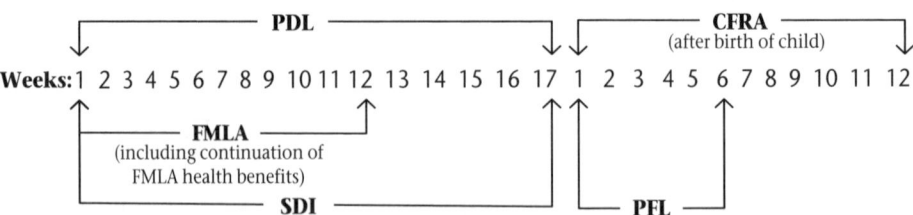

- An eligible employee may collect SDI for the duration of the time she is disabled by pregnancy, childbirth, or related medical condition, after the initial seven-day waiting period for benefits to begin;

- If the employee receives SDI benefits (after the initial seven-day waiting period), there is no additional seven-day waiting period before PFL benefits begin;

- An eligible employee may collect PFL benefits for a maximum of 6 weeks in a 12-month period to bond with a new child;

- PFL tax began January 1, 2004, although actual benefits payments for leave did not begin until July 1, 2004;

- During PDL/FMLA, you may require the use of paid sick leave and permit the use of paid vacation. The receipt of sick pay will impact the amount of SDI benefits; the use of paid vacation will not; and

- FMLA/CFRA requires that eligible employees be provided with continuation of health benefits as if the employee were still at work and on the payroll. Employees get one 12-week period of continued health benefits in each 12-month period. The leave does not have to be taken concurrently to retain health benefits.

State Disability Insurance (SDI)

An employee on PDL may be eligible for SDI benefits during the time she is disabled by the pregnancy. SDI benefits are limited to the time the employee is actually disabled, and do not include payments during periods of baby bonding. For more information, see Chapter 6, "SDI and PFL."

Paid Family Leave (PFL)

PFL benefits are intended to compensate employees who must care for a family member, or who wish to bond with a new child. The employee on PDL would not be eligible for PFL benefits while disabled by pregnancy. However, she could apply for up to six weeks of PFL benefits once she is no longer disabled, and while she is bonding with the new child.

If the employee applies for PFL benefits after her disability ends, you may require her to use up to two weeks of accrued vacation, if available. PFL benefits are not a total wage replacement. You may supplement PFL benefits with sick pay. You may not require your employee to use more sick pay than necessary to provide 100 percent of her regular wages.

Most California employees are eligible for SDI and PFL benefits. PFL benefits became available July 1, 2004. For more information, see Chapter 6, "SDI and PFL."

SDI and Workers' Compensation

While it is possible that a pregnant employee could suffer a work-related illness or injury that puts her health or that of her child in jeopardy, the employee would not receive payments from SDI and workers' compensation concurrently. The employee's health care provider determines whether the employee is disabled by pregnancy, childbirth or a related medical condition, in which case she might be eligible for SDI payments. Your workers' compensation doctor makes the determination as to whether the employee suffered a work-related illness or injury, in which case she is eligible for workers' compensation payments.

Continuing Benefits

This section discusses your obligations to continue your employee's benefits while she is using PDL.

The Law Explained

The law does not require you to continue benefits for an employee on PDL unless:

- You continue such benefits for employees on other types of disability leave (for example, you have a policy or practice allowing employees who are absent for other reasons to continue health insurance coverage for the month in which they become disabled or unable to work); or

- You have more than 50 employees, and are covered by FMLA/CFRA. In this case, you must continue to provide health benefits as if the employee were still actively at work.

Employers Covered by PDL Only

Employees who are on PDL retain employee status during the disability leave period. The leave does not constitute a break in service for purposes of longevity or seniority under any collective bargaining agreement or under any employee benefit plan.

During PDL, the employee is entitled to certain benefits, to the same extent and under the same conditions as would apply to any other unpaid disability leave for any reason other than pregnancy.[3]

The employee on PDL will continue to:

- Accrue seniority; and
- Participate in:
  - Health plans;
  - Employee benefit plans (including life, short-term and long-term disability, and accident insurance);
  - Pension and retirement plans; and
  - Supplemental unemployment benefit plans.

---

3. Pregnancy Discrimination Act, 42 U.S.C. 2000(k)

If your policy allows seniority to accrue when employees are on paid leave (such as paid sick or vacation leave) or unpaid leave, then seniority will accrue during any part of a paid or unpaid PDL, consistent with your policy.

Employers Covered by PDL and FMLA/CFRA

If your company has more than 50 employees, and your employee is eligible for FMLA/CFRA leave, see "Continuing Benefits" in Chapter 3, page 62.

What You Should Do

What you should do regarding continuation of benefits during PDL depends on whether you are also covered by FMLA/CFRA.

Employers Covered by PDL Only

If you have fewer than 50 employees, or the employee is not eligible for FMLA:

1. In your employee handbook (if you have one), include a statement in your PDL policy regarding whether you continue benefits during PDL. If you continue employee-paid benefits, also include a statement that the employee is required to continue paying for those benefits during the leave.

2. At the time the leave begins, provide the employee with written notice as to which benefits you provide, and, if applicable, the amount the employee must pay for those benefits and how/when she must make those payments in order for her benefits to continue.

3. Have the employee sign a notice acknowledging she will not continue receiving benefits if she does not make the payments for continued benefits.

4. If your employee health plan is ERISA qualified, advise employees in your written policy or employee handbook the length of time coverage remains in effect for any type of absence. The sample *Leaves of Absence Policy*, described in Table 16 on page 97, contains optional language you can use for this purpose.

5. Send a timely notice to the employee concerning Cal-COBRA/COBRA rights after the continuation of health benefits expire. For information on COBRA and the forms that may be necessary, see "COBRA and Cal-COBRA" in Chapter 1, page 12.

Employers Covered by PDL and FMLA/CFRA

If you have more than 50 employees, you must continue providing benefits during PDL as if the employee was still at work. For more information, see "Continuing Benefits" in Chapter 3, page 62.

Handling the Employee's Return to Work

When your employee is released to return to work, she will either return to the job she held before her leave, or she will take leave under CFRA for baby bonding, if eligible. If the employee chooses to take baby-bonding leave under CFRA, then her rights to reinstatement at the end of that leave are governed by CFRA regulations. For more information, see "Handling the Employee's Return to Work" in Chapter 3, page 64.

The Law Explained

Under most circumstances, you must reinstate an employee returning from PDL to the same job she held before the leave, with no less seniority than she had when her PDL began. This includes seniority for the purposes of layoff, recall, promotion, job assignment, and seniority-related benefits such as vacation.

You must resume benefits upon the employee's reinstatement in the same manner, and at the same levels, as provided when the leave began, without any new qualification period, physical exam, etc.

You may require medical certification of the employee's ability to return to her previously held job, including the date that she can return. You can use the *Certification of Physician or Practitioner for Employee Return to Work*, described in Table 8 on page 35, to obtain this certification. Keep the form in the employee's confidential medical file, separate from her personnel file.

- If the employee is not released to return to work before the leave expires, you must treat the employee the same as you treat any other similarly situated employee regarding reinstatement.

- If an employee returning from PDL, FMLA, or CFRA is disabled by an injury or illness that is not related to the pregnancy or childbirth, she may be entitled to reasonable accommodation. For more information, see Chapter 4, "Disability Leave."

An employee who has recently given birth may request to return to a different job or a different schedule. An employee returning from PDL is not entitled to any special consideration for such requests. Treat her request the same as you would any other employee request for a change in hours or position.

Reinstatement to a Comparable Position

If you do not reinstate the employee to her same position, you still may have an obligation to return her to a comparable position that:

- Involves the same or substantially similar duties and responsibilities;
- Requires equivalent skills, effort, and authority;
- Is virtually identical to the employee's former position in terms of pay, benefits, privileges, fringe benefits, and status.

A comparable position is one that:

- Is open on the employee's scheduled return date or within 10 days of reinstatement;
- The employee is qualified to perform; and
- The employee is entitled to have by company policy, contract, or collective bargaining agreement.

Refusing Reinstatement

You may refuse reinstatement, but only in very limited circumstances.

You can refuse to reinstate an employee if you can show that you cannot restore her to the same or a comparable position. This requires that either no comparable position is available or filling an available comparable position with the returning employee would substantially undermine your ability to operate your business safely and efficiently.

If you plan to refuse reinstatement to an employee on PDL, or if you plan to lay off an employee on PDL, consult with legal counsel before taking any action.

Employee Layoffs

You can justify refusing to reinstate an employee if you can prove that you would have laid off the employee regardless of whether she was on PDL or not. This may be difficult to prove — you must have documented proof that you would have laid off the employee based on:

- Seniority;
- Position;
- Department; or
- Other non-discriminatory factors (such as documented performance issues).

Business Need

You can justify refusing to reinstate the employee to her same, or an equivalent, position if there is substantial business need — in other words preserving the employee's job would undermine your ability to run your business safely and efficiently.

This position is extremely difficult to prove. The following circumstances are invalid defenses:

- You distributed the job duties of the employee on PDL to several other employees and found that they could handle the additional workload;
- You hired a temporary employee as a substitute for your employee on PDL, and found that the temporary employee does a better job;
- You had to lay-off one person from a department, and selected the employee on PDL because she was already out of the workplace; and
- You have heard, through other employees, or even the disabled employee herself, that she was considering not returning to work at the end of her leave.

Lactation Accommodation

An employee who is breast feeding and needs to express milk is entitled to accommodation. Time taken by a non-exempt employee is unpaid, unless taken during a paid break. Any time in excess of the break may be unpaid. You cannot deduct increments of less than a complete day from the salary of an exempt employee.

You must provide a private room or other location, in close proximity to the employee's work area. This location cannot be a toilet stall. However, it may be the employee's work area, if it is private.

What You Should Do

Reinstating an employee from pregnancy disability leave to her job is generally a straightforward process. Before she returns to work, you should:

1. Require medical certification that the employee is fit to return to work.

2. Designate a private location for accommodating her need to express breast milk.

3. Notify the payroll department of the date the employee is resuming work so that it can reactivate her regular paycheck.

Forms and Checklists

New for 2005 The following table describes forms associated with PDL.

 You can find these forms on the CD included with this product.

Table 8. Forms and Checklists

Form name	What do I use it for?	When do I use it?	Who fills it out?	Where does it go?
California Family Rights Act and Pregnancy Disability Poster (English)	To inform employees about their rights and benefits. Required if you have 50 or more employees.	Display at all times. Provide a copy when you learn of an employee's pregnancy or she inquires about PDL or a PDL-related transfer.	No filling out needed.	Display in a conspicuous location visible to all employees. Give a copy to the pregnant employee (required). Give a copy to any employee on FMLA/CFRA leave (optional).

Table 8. Forms and Checklists *(continued)*

Form name	What do I use it for?	When do I use it?	Who fills it out?	Where does it go?
California Family Rights Act and Pregnancy Disability Poster (Spanish)	To inform Spanish-speaking employees of their rights and benefits. Required if you have 50 or more employees and 10 percent or more of your workforce speaks Spanish as a primary language.	Display at all times. Provide a copy when you learn of an employee's pregnancy or she inquires about PDL or a PDL-related transfer.	No filling out needed.	Display in a conspicuous location visible to all employees. Give a copy to the pregnant employee (required). Give a copy to any employee on FMLA/CFRA leave (optional).
Certification of Physician or Practitioner for Employee Return to Work	To obtain physician or medical practitioner certification that the employee is fit to return to work.	Before allowing an employee on to return to work from a medically related leave (PDL, FMLA/CFRA, disability, or workers' compensation).	Employee's physician or medical practitioner.	In the employee's confidential medical file, separate from his/her personnel file.
Certification of Physician or Practitioner for PDL or PDL/FMLA	To obtain physician or medical practitioner certification that the employee is disabled due to pregnancy.	When the employee requests PDL.	Employee's physician or medical practitioner.	In the employee's confidential medical file, separate from her personnel file.
Certification of Physician or Practitioner for Transfer Due to Pregnancy Disability	To obtain physician or medical practitioner certification that the employee requires a transfer due to pregnancy.	When the employee requests a PDL-related transfer.	Employee's physician or medical practitioner.	In the employee's confidential medical file, separate from her personnel file.

Table 8. Forms and Checklists *(continued)*

Form name	What do I use it for?	When do I use it?	Who fills it out?	Where does it go?
Coordination of PDL with Family/Medical Leave Policy (50 or More Employees)	To inform employees that PDL runs concurrently with FMLA leave.	At time of hire and whenever you update the policy.	No filling out needed; you develop your policy based on this sample.	In your employee handbook; if you don't have a handbook, give a copy to every employee.
Employee Letter - CFRA Leave Taken after FMLA/PDL	To notify the employee of the type of leave that has been granted.	At the beginning of the leave.	You do.	Send to the employee. Keep a copy in the employee's confidential medical file, separate from his/her personnel file.
Employee Letter - PDL Only	To notify the employee of the type of leave that has been granted.	At the beginning of the leave.	You do.	Send to the employee. Keep a copy in the employee's confidential medical file, separate from her personnel file.
Employee Letter - PDL/FMLA	To notify the employee of the type of leave that has been granted.	At the beginning of the leave.	You do.	Send to the employee. Keep a copy in the employee's confidential medical file, separate from her personnel file.

Table 8. Forms and Checklists *(continued)*

Form name	What do I use it for?	When do I use it?	Who fills it out?	Where does it go?
Notice to Employee as to Change in Relationship	To notify an employee that the employment relationship has changed. Required for: • Discharge; • Layoff; and • Leave of absence.	At the beginning of the leave or at the time of layoff or discharge. Written notice must be provided by this form, your own form, or a letter. The notice must include: • Employer name; • Employee name; • Employee Social Security number; • Indication that the action was a discharge, layoff, leave of absence, or a change in status; and • The date of the action.	You do. You should request the employee's signature, but it is not required by law.	Give to the employee. Keep a copy in the employee's personnel record.
PDL Checklist for Employer Compliance (5–49 Employees)	To help you comply with state PDL laws.	When an employee: • Requests PDL/FMLA; or • Is absent for a PDL/FMLA qualifying reason.	You do.	In a file for all PDL leaves or in the employee's personnel file.

Table 8. Forms and Checklists *(continued)*

Form name	What do I use it for?	When do I use it?	Who fills it out?	Where does it go?
PDL Documentation - For Employer Use Only (5–49 Employees)	To document your PDL-related actions for a specific employee.	When an employee: • Requests PDL; • Requests a transfer due to pregnancy disability; or • Is absent for a PDL qualifying reason.	You do.	In a file for all PDL leaves or in the employee's personnel file.
PDL/FMLA Checklist for Employer Compliance (50 or More Employees)	To help you comply with state and federal PDL and FMLA laws.	When an employee: • Requests PDL/FMLA; or • Is absent for a PDL/FMLA qualifying reason.	You do.	In a file for all PDL leaves or in the employee's personnel file.
PDL/FMLA Documentation - For Employer Use Only (50 or More Employees)	To document your PDL/FMLA-related actions for a specific employee.	When an employee: • Requests PDL/FMLA; • Requests a transfer due to a PDL/FMLA reason; or • Is absent for a PDL/FMLA qualifying reason.	You do.	In a file for all PDL leaves or in the employee's personnel file.
Pregnancy Disability Leave Policy (5 or More Employees)	To inform employees about their rights and responsibilities under state PDL laws.	At time of hire and whenever you update the policy.	No filling out needed; you develop your policy based on this sample.	In your employee handbook; if you don't have a handbook, give a copy to every employee.

Table 8. Forms and Checklists *(continued)*

Form name	What do I use it for?	When do I use it?	Who fills it out?	Where does it go?
Pregnancy Disability Leave Poster (English)	To inform employees about their rights and benefits. Required if you have 5 or more employees.	Display at all times. Provide a copy when you learn of an employee's pregnancy or she inquires about PDL or a PDL-related transfer.	No filling out needed.	Display in a conspicuous location visible to all employees. Give a copy to the pregnant employee.
Pregnancy Disability Leave Poster (Spanish)	To inform Spanish-speaking employees of their rights and benefits.	Display at all times. Provide a copy when you learn of an employee's pregnancy or she inquires about PDL or a PDL-related transfer.	No filling out needed.	Display in a conspicuous location visible to all employees. Give a copy to the pregnant employee.
Temporary Transfers Policy	To inform employees about how your company handles requests for temporary transfers.	At time of hire and whenever you update the policy.	No filling out needed; you develop your policy based on this sample.	In your employee handbook; if you don't have a handbook, give a copy to every employee.

Further Information

You can get more information about PDL from the following resources:

- Department of Fair Employment and Housing (DFEH) at **http://www.dfeh.ca.gov/**;
- Employment Development Department (EDD) at **http://www.edd.ca.gov**; and
- California Code of Regulations at **http://ccr.oal.ca.gov**. Click the California Code of Regulations infobase link, then look up Title 2, Division 4, Chapter 2, Subchapter 6A.

Chapter 3
Family Medical Leave

If you employ 50 or more employees, you are subject to state and federal family medical leave laws. This chapter guides covered employers through common family medical leave issues.

 The forms mentioned in this chapter are on the CD included with this product.

The following table provides a broad overview of family medical leave:

Table 9. Family Medical Leave

Family medical leave issue	Requirement
Covered employers	If you employ 50 or more employees, you are covered by the federal Family and Medical Leave Act (FMLA) and the California Family Rights Act (CFRA). See "Who's Covered?" on page 43.
Maximum amount of leave	FMLA and CFRA both provide a maximum of 12 weeks of leave in a 12-month period, and, except for disabilities due to pregnancy, run concurrently.
Employee eligibility	Employees are eligible if they are employed at a worksite with 50 or more employees in a 75 mile radius. Eligible employees must also have worked for the employer for 12 months (need not be consecutive) and 1,250 hours in the 12 months prior to the need for leave. See "Who's Eligible?" on page 43.

Table 9. Family Medical Leave *(continued)*

Family medical leave issue	Requirement
Reasons for leave	An employee may use FMLA/CFRA in the following three circumstances: • His/her own serious illness or injury; • To care for a seriously ill family member; or • Baby bonding. **New for 2005** An employee in a registered domestic partnership is not entitled to FMLA to care for his/her domestic partner, but is entitled to CFRA for that purpose. See "What's a Qualifying Event?" on page 44 and "Domestic Partners and CFRA" on page 56.
Employer responsibilities	When you learn that an employee is absent for any reason that may qualify as FMLA/CFRA, you should send a notice to the employee, designating any time off related to the absence as FMLA/CFRA. There are also requirements for posters and notices. See "Required Posters and Notices" on page 47.
Interaction with other leaves	These are numerous, and somewhat complicated. See "Controlling Family Medical Leave" on page 53.
Ending the employment relationship before the leave expires	The employee has no greater rights than if he or she were not out on leave. The right to reinstatement would end if the employment relationship ends. However, employees on FMLA/CFRA are protected from retaliation for taking leave. Consult with your legal counsel before you terminate an employee on FMLA/CFRA. See "Handling the Employee's Return to Work" on page 64.

The following checklists can help you audit your FMLA/CFRA leave-related compliance activities, with reminders of key milestones in the process. Have copies nearby as you work through this chapter, noting completed activities and steps you have yet to take or develop.

- *PDL/FMLA Checklist for Employer Compliance (50 or More Employees)*, described in Table 8 on page 39;
- *PDL/FMLA Documentation - For Employer Use Only (50 or More Employees)*, described in Table 8 on page 39; and
- *FMLA/CFRA Checklist for Employer Compliance*, described in Table 10 on page 69.

Family Medical Leave Defined

The federal Family and Medical Leave Act (FMLA) and its California counterpart, the California Family Rights Act of 1993 (CFRA), each provide eligible employees with the right to an unpaid leave of absence for up to 12 weeks within a 12-month period, for a qualifying reason. Except for pregnancy disability leave (PDL) and leave to care for a registered domestic partner, FMLA and CFRA leaves run concurrently. For more information on FMLA and CFRA as they relate to PDL, see Chapter 2, "Pregnancy Disability Leave." For more information on CFRA leave for domestic partners, see "Domestic Partners and CFRA" on page 56.

Who's Covered?

State and federal family medical leave laws cover private employers with 50 or more employees on their payroll during any 20 or more calendar weeks in the current or preceding calendar year. This includes employees on the payroll who received no compensation, part-time employees, commissioned employees, and employees on leave who are expected to return to active employment. Employees on layoff do not count.

You remain covered by FMLA/CFRA even when your employee count falls below 50 employees. In order to lose FMLA/CFRA coverage, you must employ less than 50 employees for 20 workweeks in the current and preceding year. These workweeks need not be consecutive.

Who's Eligible?

Working for a covered employer does not automatically make an employee eligible for FMLA/CFRA leave. An employee is eligible for family medical leave if he/she:

- Works for a covered employer;
- Has worked for that employer for at least 12 months (the 12 months do not have to be consecutive);
- Has worked for the employer for at least 1,250 hours in the past 12 months; and
- Works at a worksite where the employer employs 50 or more employees either at the worksite or within 75 road miles of the worksite.

You could be covered by FMLA/CFRA, but have no employees that are eligible for FMLA/CFRA leave.

Example: You have 30 employees in San Diego, 30 in Santa Barbara, and 30 in San Francisco. Although you have a total of 90 employees and you are a covered employer, no employees are eligible for family medical leave because no one location has 50 employees within a 75-mile radius. You are still obligated to post the family medical leave poster, but you may deny family medical leave to your employees.

The eligibility requirement for an employee who takes CFRA leave for baby bonding is different than for an employee who takes FMLA/CFRA or PDL/FMLA. The 12-month period during which the employee (taking CFRA only) must have worked 1,250 hours is the period immediately preceding her first day of PDL/FMLA leave, based on her pregnancy disability. She does not have to meet the 1,250 hour eligibility requirement a second time before taking CFRA for baby bonding.

What's a Qualifying Event?

An employee may take family medical leave under the following general circumstances:

- To address his/her own serious health condition;

- To care for a child, parent, spouse, or registered domestic partner with a serious health condition; or

- To bond with a new baby.

Serious Health Conditions and Family Care

An employee may use FMLA/CFRA leave for his/her own serious health condition. He/she may also use family medical leave to care for a child, parent, or spouse who has a serious health condition.

New for 2005 An employee may use CFRA leave to care for a registered domestic partner who has a serious health condition. See "California Domestic Partner Rights and Responsibilities Act" in Chapter 1, page 10, and "Domestic Partners and CFRA" on page 56.

A serious health condition is defined as an illness, injury, impairment, or physical or mental condition that involves either:

- Inpatient care (for example, an overnight stay) in a hospital, hospice, or residential medical care facility; or

- Continuing treatment by, or under the supervision of, a health care provider.

A serious health condition involving continuing treatment by a health care provider includes any one or more of the following:

- A period of incapacity (inability to work, attend school, or perform other regular daily activities) of more than three consecutive calendar days, and any subsequent treatment or period of incapacity relating to the same condition, that also involves:
    - Treatment two or more times by a health care provider nurse or physician's assistant under orders of, or on referral by, a health care provider; or
    - Treatment by a health care provider on at least one occasion, which results in a regimen of continuing treatment under the supervision of the health care provider.
- Any period of incapacity due to pregnancy, or for prenatal care;
- Any period of incapacity or treatment for such incapacity due to a chronic serious health conditions — requiring periodic visits for treatment by a health care provider or nurse/physician's assistant under direct supervision of a health care provider, which continues over an extended period of time (including recurring episodes of a single underlying condition); and may cause episodic rather than a continuing period of incapacity (i.e. asthma, diabetes, or epilepsy);
- A period of incapacity that is permanent or long-term due to a condition for which treatment may not be effective (for example, Alzheimer's, a severe stroke, or the terminal stages of a disease); or
- Any period of absence to receive multiple treatments (and any recovery from the treatments) by a health care provider or under the direction of a health care provider, either for restorative surgery after an accident or other injury, or for a condition that would likely result in a period of incapacity of more than three consecutive calendar days in the absence of medical intervention or treatment (for example, chemotherapy or radiation for a cancer patient).

Baby Bonding

Baby bonding includes leave for an employee, either male or female, to bond with his/her own child, or with his/her adopted or foster child. All leave for baby bonding must conclude within one year of the birth of the child, or one year from the date the child was placed with the employee for adoption or foster care.

The 12 Week Maximum

Employees can use federal or state family medical leave for a maximum combined total of 12 weeks in a 12-month period. Twelve weeks is defined as the equivalent of 12 normally scheduled workweeks. Employees who work more or less than five days a week, or who work an alternative work schedule, receive leave on a pro-rata or proportional basis of 12 weeks.

Example: If your full-time employee works five eight-hour days every week, 12 workweeks equals 60 working days of leave entitlement. For the employee who works half-time, 12 workweeks might mean:

- 30 eight-hour days;
- 60 four-hour days; or
- 12 workweeks of whatever is the employee's normal half-time work schedule.

If an employee takes leave on an intermittent or reduced work schedule, you may only count the amount of leave actually taken toward the 12 weeks of leave.

Example: If an employee needs physical therapy requiring two hours of absence each week, you may only charge the employee with two hours of family medical leave for each week.

If the FMLA leave is running concurrently with PDL, the overall duration of the leave may extend to beyond a total of 12 weeks. See "Handling Employee Requests" on page 48.

Defining a 12-Month Period

You can use a number of different methods to determine the 12-month period in which the 12 workweeks of leave entitlement occur:

1. A calendar year;

2. Any fixed 12-month leave year, such as a fiscal year, or a year starting on an employee's anniversary date;

3. The 12-month period measured forward from the date an employee's first family medical leave begins; or

4. A "rolling" 12-month period measured backward from the date an employee uses any family medical leave.

Under methods 1 and 2, an employee is entitled to up to 12 workweeks of family leave at any time in the fixed 12-month period. An employee could take 12 workweeks of leave at the end of the year, and 12 workweeks at the beginning of the following year, creating the potential for 24 straight workweeks of leave.

Under method 3, an employee is entitled to 12 workweeks of leave during the year beginning on the first date family medical leave is taken. The next 12-month period begins the first time family medical leave is taken after completion of any previous 12-month period.

Under method 4, the rolling 12-month period, each time an employee takes family leave, the remaining leave entitlement is any balance of the 12 workweeks not used during the immediately preceding 12 months.

> **Example:** If an employee has taken 8 workweeks of leave during the previous 12 months, he/she still has four workweeks of leave.
>
> Or, if an employee uses four workweeks beginning February 1, 2005, four workweeks beginning June 1, 2005, and four workweeks beginning December 2, 2005, the employee is not entitled to any additional leave until February 1, 2006. However, beginning on February 1, 2006, the employee is entitled to four workweeks of leave; on June 1, 2006, the employee is entitled to an additional four workweeks, and on December 2, 2006 will have recovered his/her full 12 weeks.

Methods 3 and 4 offer employers the greatest control over the time an employee is away on family medical leave. These two choices prevent employees from taking two 12-week leaves back-to-back, or in a time period of less than 12 months.

You must apply your chosen method consistently and uniformly to all employees. Explain the method you choose in the FMLA/CFRA policy in your employee handbook. If you do not clearly explain your calculation method to employees, you must give them whichever method provides the most family medical leave time, as courts will apply the option most favorable to the employee.[4]

Required Posters and Notices

Employers of 50 or more employees must post two notices:

- *California Family Rights Act and Pregnancy Disability Poster;* and
- *Federal Family and Medical Leave Act Poster.*

If you have Spanish-speaking employees, you may need to display posters in both English and Spanish. For more information on these posters, see Table 8 on page 35 and Table 10 on page 68.

---

4. *Bachelder v. America West Airlines,* 259 F.3rd 1112 (2001)

All posters must be displayed in a conspicuous place that is frequented by your employees (such as a break room or cafeteria).

You are encouraged to give a copy of the *California Family Rights Act and Pregnancy Disability Poster* to an employee who is on FMLA/CFRA leave, but there is no requirement that you do so. However, if the reason for the leave is related to pregnancy disability, you must provide a copy of this poster to the employee who is taking PDL/FMLA leave. For information on other forms you must give to an employee taking PDL, see Table 10 on page 68.

The California Chamber of Commerce produces an all-in-one **Employer Poster** that contains all the required employer postings, in both English and Spanish. For more information, call (800) 331-8877 or visit our online store at *http://www.calchamberstore.com*.

Handling Employee Requests

This section explains the laws you must follow and tasks you should perform when an employee requests time off for family medical leave.

The Law Explained

Once an employee gives you notice of the need for FMLA/CFRA leave, you must respond to the request within one or two business days if feasible, or within a "reasonable time" after the employee provides you with notice. The law does not define "reasonable time," but you should not delay in responding to an employee request for mandated leave. If an employee has taken leave for a pregnancy-related disability, and is taking additional leave under CFRA for baby bonding, you must respond verbally within one or two business days to her request for CFRA leave. You must respond in writing no later than 10 calendar days after you receive it.

Although the FMLA/CFRA laws require employees to provide at least 30 days verbal notice prior to the leave, this rule will not apply in many cases.

> **Example:** An eligible employee who is pregnant has provided certification from her doctor stating the anticipated delivery date. Two months prior to the birth of her child, the employee is ordered to complete bed rest for the duration of the pregnancy. Ultimately, the employee's health care provider, or the employee's need for immediate treatment, may make the prior notice impossible. In this case, the employee must notify you as soon as practicable.

Although the employee does not have to specifically mention FMLA or CFRA by name, he/she must provide enough information to validate that the leave qualifies as FMLA/CFRA.

See "What's a Qualifying Event?" on page 44 to help identify the circumstances that trigger the designation. If the employee fails or refuses to provide enough information to enable you to make such a determination, you may deny his/her request for leave.

However, if an employee requests to use paid leave for an FMLA/CFRA qualifying purpose, but does not explain the reason for the leave (consistent with your established policy or practice), and you deny the leave, the employee must provide sufficient information to establish an FMLA/CFRA qualifying reason. Once the employee provides enough information to validate the need for FMLA/CFRA, you may then count the leave, paid or unpaid, against the employee's 12-week entitlement.

An employee who uses paid leave, then seeks an unpaid extension for an FMLA/CFRA qualifying event must state the reason for the extension. If the extension is for an event that occurred during the period of paid leave, you may count the leave used after the FMLA-qualifying event against the employee's 12-week entitlement.

An employee may waive his/her right to FMLA/CFRA. If an employee refuses to provide certification of the need for leave, you have no obligation to provide it. Or, if an employee resigns and refuses to give you enough information about the need for leave, he/she has waived his/her rights to FMLA.

> **Example:** If an employee wishes to maintain complete confidentiality about the reason for his/her absences, and refuses to provide certification for FMLA/CFRA, you have no obligation to advise the employee further of his/her FMLA/CFRA rights.

You should carefully document the employee's refusal, and consult with legal counsel. With your attorney, discuss sending written notice to the employee that his/her failure to comply with the certification process has resulted in a denial of FMLA/CFRA rights.

If an employee requests additional leave for the same reason as the first leave, he/she does not need to meet the eligibility tests again to requalify for additional leave within the 12-month period. The employee is entitled to take additional leave for the same reason as the first leave, even if there are now fewer than 50 employees at his/her worksite or within a 75-mile radius.

If the additional leave is for a different reason than the original leave, the employee must requalify (for example, first six weeks of leave was for care of a newborn, and additional leave is requested for the employee's own illness).

Once you know that a leave is for an FMLA/CFRA qualifying reason, you are responsible for notifying the employee that the leave will count as such. It is also your responsibility to inquire further about the need for FMLA/CFRA leave when an employee is absent.

 A federal court held that an employer who is aware of a change in an employee's behavior has sufficient notice of the employee's need for FMLA leave.[5] In this case, an employee suffering from depression was unable to express the need for FMLA leave. In concluding that the symptoms and behavior associated with the depression were sufficient to put the employer on notice of the employee's need for FMLA, the court noted that an employee does not need to ask for FMLA by name when he/she collapses at work as the result of a stroke, heart attack, or insulin deficiency.

Obtaining Medical Certification

You may require medical certification for the need for FMLA/CFRA leave, if the leave is for the employee's own illness or injury or to care for a family member. Medical certification is not required for CFRA leave taken for baby bonding.

New for 2005 You may require medical certification for the need for CFRA leave to care for a registered domestic partner, but only if you require certification for other family members.

 Medical certification for family medical leave purposes means a written communication from the health care provider of the child, parent, spouse, domestic partner, or employee with a serious health condition.

Certification of medical leave for the employee's own serious health condition must contain:

- The date, if known, on which the serious health condition commenced;
- The probable duration of the condition; and
- A statement that, due to the serious health condition, the employee is unable to work at all or is unable to perform any one or more of the essential functions of his/her position.

Privacy laws limit the type of information you may require on such certification. The medical certification form provided by the US Department of Labor (DOL), *Certification of Health Care Provider – WH 380*, requests medical facts to support the certification. California law prohibits the release of such information by a health care provider, unless the patient signs a valid waver of his/her right to privacy. The *Medical*

---

5. *Byrne v. Aron Products, Inc.*, 328 F.3rd 379 (7th Cir. 2003)

Certification - FMLA/CFRA form, on the CD included with this product, is appropriate for use in California.

 A **health care provider** is a physician, surgeon, nurse practitioner, nurse midwife, or other person capable of providing health care services. The health care provider can be licensed in the United States or any other country.

If the family care leave is for the employee's child, parent, spouse, or registered domestic partner, the certification need not identify the serious health condition involved, but must contain:

- The date, if known, on which the serious health condition commenced;
- The probable duration of the condition;
- An estimate of the amount of time which the health care provider believes the employee needs to care for the child, parent, spouse, or registered domestic partner; and
- A statement that the serious health condition warrants the employee's participation in providing care during a period of treatment, or supervision of the child, parent, spouse, or registered domestic partner. This includes, but is not limited to:
  - Providing psychological comfort;
  - Arranging "third party" care for the child, parent, spouse, or registered domestic partner; and
  - Directly providing, or participating in, the medical care.

There are no provisions in the family leave regulations that allow you to request more information or challenge the validity of a certification for the employee's family member. You must accept the certification provided.

When an employee seeks family leave to care for an ill family member, you may not require the employee to prove that no other caretakers are available.

You may require the employee to provide medical certification within 15 calendar days of your request for certification. However, if it is not practicable for the employee to do so despite his/her good faith efforts, the leave may begin before you receive the certification.

You may terminate an employee who refuses to provide the required medical certification, and who remains absent from work. Apply a consistent process in dealing with unauthorized absences from work.

What You Should Do

1. Require your employee to provide at least 30 days notice before he/she takes FMLA/CFRA leave. You can use the following forms to help with the process:

   - *Employee Letter - PDL Only*, described in Table 8 on page 37;
   - *Employee Letter - PDL/FMLA*, described in Table 8 on page 37;
   - *Employee Letter - FMLA/CFRA*, described in Table 10 on page 68;
   - *Employee Letter - CFRA Leave Taken after FMLA/PDL*, described in Table 8 on page 37; and
   - *Request for Use of Kin Care*, described in Table 21 on page 120.

   Send a copy to the employee and keep a copy in the employee's confidential medical file.

2. Provide the appropriate notices to the employee who is pregnant and eligible for PDL/FMLA and CFRA and the employee who is eligible for FMLA/CFRA. Notices required by law include:

   - *California Family Rights Act and Pregnancy Disability Poster*; and
   - *Federal Family and Medical Leave Act Poster*.

3. Provide the appropriate pamphlets to the employee who is pregnant and eligible for PDL/FMLA and CFRA and the employee who is eligible for FMLA/CFRA. Notices required by law include:

   - *State Disability Insurance Provisions (DE 2515)* if you are designating the leave as FMLA/CFRA for the employee's own health condition; and
   - *Paid Family Leave (DE 2511)* if the leave is:
     - FMLA/CFRA leave to bond with a new child or to care for a parent, spouse, or dependant child; or
     - CFRA leave to care for a registered domestic partner.

4. Use the *Medical Certification - FMLA/CFRA* form to obtain physician or medical practitioner verification that the employee qualifies for the leave. Keep a copy of this form in the employee's confidential medical file.

   If the employee requests additional leave upon expiration of the period that the health care provider originally estimated, you may require him/her to obtain recertification.

   If you doubt the validity of the medical certification for an employee taking family leave for his/her own serious health condition, you may require the employee to obtain, at your expense, the opinion of a second health care provider, designated or approved by you, concerning any information in the certification. You cannot employ your designated or approved health care provider on a regular basis.

If the second opinion differs from the opinion in the original certification, you may require the employee to obtain, at your expense, the opinion of a third health care provider, designated or approved by both you and the employee, concerning any information in the certification. The opinion of the third health care provider is final and is binding to both you and the employee.

Any medical information you receive regarding an employee is subject to confidentiality laws. Keep this information in a confidential medical file separate from the employee's regular personnel file.

5. Complete a *Notice to Employee as to Change in Relationship*, described in Table 8 on page 38, to document the employee's leave of absence at the time leave begins (if for the employee's own serious health condition).

6. Manage the leave of absence process using:

- *FMLA/CFRA Checklist for Employer Compliance* if an employee is absent for a reason that may qualify as PDL/FMLA or FMLA/CFRA;

- *PDL/FMLA Documentation - For Employer Use Only (50 or More Employees)* when the employee is eligible for FMLA/CFRA; and

- *PDL/FMLA Checklist for Employer Compliance (50 or More Employees)*.

You can find these forms on the CD included with this product.

Controlling Family Medical Leave

Controlling family medical leave begins with recognizing a qualifying event (either because the employee tells you or you learn some other way), and then notifying the employee that you are placing him/her on FMLA/CFRA leave. By providing notice that you are designating the leave as FMLA/CFRA, you start counting the absences against the legally mandated 12-week entitlement and any additional leave you choose to provide by policy.

Controlling family medical leave also involves coordinating leave entitlements with your own voluntary policies of allowing or requiring other forms of leave. As we have suggested earlier, leaves of absence can occur either one after the other (as with CFRA leave, which can begin only after pregnancy disability ends), or overlapping, (as with pregnancy disability leave and FMLA leave, which run concurrently). Running leaves of absence concurrently with one another, where allowed by law or by your policy, is a key tool in helping you manage the overall amount of time an employee is away from work.

The Law Explained

For purposes of FMLA and CFRA, an eligible employee is entitled to a maximum of 12 weeks in a 12-month period. The two leaves run concurrently, except in the case of pregnancy-related disability.

Pregnancy Disability and FMLA/CFRA

Pregnancy-related disabilities are covered by FMLA. Therefore, such leaves of absence are charged to an employee's FMLA entitlement. Pregnancy-related disabilities are not, however, covered by CFRA. Rights of employees disabled by pregnancy-related conditions are discussed in more detail in Chapter 2, "Pregnancy Disability Leave."

In summary:

- The PDL entitlement is 4 months, or 17 weeks plus 3, or 88 working days, or 704 hours, of which 12 weeks, or 60 days, or 480 hours is concurrent with FMLA; and

- The CFRA entitlement, taken after a PDL/FMLA leave (because CFRA and PDL do not run concurrently), is 3 months, or 12 weeks, or 60 working days, or 480 hours. CFRA leave may be taken for purposes of bonding with the baby, but not during the period of pregnancy-related disability.

Here are two timelines, which help illustrate the relationship between the three mandated leaves. The first shows the maximum 17 weeks of PDL, with the maximum 12 weeks of FMLA running concurrently, followed by the period of CFRA entitlement.

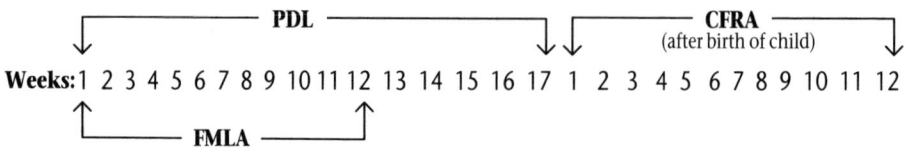

The second timeline shows a more common scenario, as when an employee's pregnancy disability is shorter than the 12-week FMLA entitlement. In this case, the CFRA entitlement runs concurrently with the FMLA entitlement for a period of four weeks.

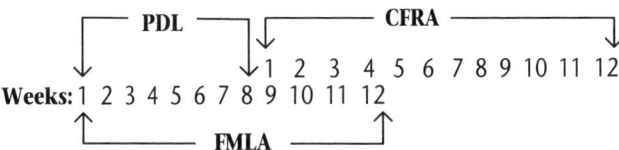

Baby Bonding after PDL/FMLA

After the birth of his/her child, your employee (either parent) is entitled to use up to 12 weeks of leave to bond with the child (see "The 12 Week Maximum" on page 45). If the female employee has given birth, but has not been released to return to work, and her disability will continue beyond the 88 working days of PDL entitlement, she may take CFRA for purposes of baby bonding.

> ***Example:*** A pregnant employee uses 40 days of PDL/FMLA before the birth of her child. After giving birth, she is still considered disabled for another 48 days. She exhausts her FMLA after a total of 60 working days and her PDL after a total of 88 working days. Because the employee has already delivered her child, she may use up to 12 weeks of CFRA leave for baby bonding.

If the employee in the above example had not yet given birth, but was disabled beyond the 88 days of PDL/FMLA, you would have no obligation to provide additional leave or job protection. However, you must treat pregnancy disability the same as other types of disability. If you gave another employee six months of leave to recover from a heart attack, you must provide the same amount of leave to an employee disabled by pregnancy.

If you employ both parents who are eligible for CFRA, you may limit the CFRA leave to a total of 12 workweeks in a 12-month period between the two parents. This limit applies to CFRA leave taken for the birth, adoption, or foster care placement of a child.

Intermittent Leave

Employees may take all 12 weeks of leave at once, or may take leave in shorter increments of hours, days, or weeks. There are, however, a few restrictions:

- Minimum duration of intermittent leave for serious health condition of employee or for care of family member. You may limit leave increments to the shortest period that your payroll system uses to account for absences or use of leave.

> ***Example:*** If employees must use vacation or sick time in half-hour increments or more, then you may require an employee leaving 20 minutes before the end of the workday for treatment for a serious health condition to use a half-hour of his/her family leave entitlement.

- Minimum duration of intermittent leave for baby bonding. The basic minimum duration of the leave is two weeks. However, you must grant a request for a family leave of less than two weeks duration on any two occasions. All leave for baby bonding must conclude within one year of the birth of the child, or one year from the date the child was placed with the employee for adoption or foster care.

Domestic Partners and CFRA

New for 2005 FMLA does not provide domestic partners with leave. However, in California, registered domestic partners have the same legal rights as a spouse, effective January 1, 2005. Therefore, an eligible employee would be entitled to up to 12 weeks of leave that is CFRA only, to care for his/her domestic partner. This does not affect the employee's FMLA entitlement. For more on domestic partners, see "California Domestic Partner Rights and Responsibilities Act" in Chapter 1, page 10.

Potential for Discrimination

In one circumstance, the new state law appears to provide registered domestic partners with more leave than single or married employees.

If, before taking any FMLA leave, a registered domestic partner takes CFRA leave (up to 12 weeks) to care for his/her domestic partner, he/she would still have 12 weeks of FMLA leave available during that 12-month period. The employee could then use FMLA leave to care for his/her own serious health condition or that of a parent or child.

In contrast, a married employee who takes leave to care for a spouse is entitled to the same 12 weeks of CFRA leave, but it runs concurrently with FMLA leave because a spouse is covered under FMLA. If that married employee later needs leave to care for his/her own serious health condition or that of a parent or child, he/she is not entitled to any more leave in the same 12-month period. This creates the potential for a claim of discrimination on the basis of marital status — because the individual is married, he/she is denied a benefit that is available to a registered domestic partner.

Your company could voluntarily remedy this by providing additional leave to the married employee whose first absence is to care for a spouse, and who then needs additional time to care for his/her own serious health condition or that of a parent or child.

> The new legislation's effect on FMLA rights for married couples is an unsettled area of the law. Consult legal counsel before granting or denying FMLA leave or an additional leave of absence to any employee.

Designating FMLA and Paid Leave

If you require the use of paid leave during FMLA/CFRA, or if you require that the employee on current paid leave counts the time as FMLA/CFRA, you must notify the employee no later than two business days after the employee gives you notice of the need for leave.

You must decide within two days if:

- You require your employee to substitute paid leave for unpaid leave; or
- You designate paid leave under an existing leave plan as FMLA/CFRA leave.

You must make your designation before the leave starts, unless you do not have sufficient information on the employee's reason for taking the leave until after the leave commences.

If you have enough information to determine that the paid leave is for an FMLA/CFRA reason, but fail to designate the leave as FMLA/CFRA leave, you may not retroactively designate leave as FMLA/CFRA. You may only designate FMLA/CFRA leave beginning on the date that you give the employee notice of the designation.

In these circumstances, the employee is subject to the full protection of family medical leave law, but you cannot count any of the absences preceding the employee's leave designation notice against the employee's 12-week FMLA/CFRA entitlement.

If you know the reason for the leave, but are unable to confirm that the leave qualifies under FMLA/CFRA, or you have requested medical certification that has not yet been provided, or you are in the process of obtaining a second or third medical opinion, you should make a preliminary designation — and notify the employee you are doing so — at the time leave begins, or as soon as the reason for the leave becomes known. When you receive either the required information from the employee or the medical certification confirming the leave is for an FMLA/CFRA reason, the preliminary designation becomes final. If the medical certification fails to confirm that the reason for the absence was an FMLA/CFRA reason, you must withdraw the designation, and notify the employee in writing.

Designating FMLA and Unpaid Leave

If an employee wishes to take unpaid leave as FMLA/CFRA, he/she must explain the reason(s) for the need for leave in enough detail to allow you to determine whether the leave qualifies as FMLA/CFRA. If the employee fails to explain the reasons, you may deny the leave.

The employee does not need to request FMLA/CFRA specifically in order to assert his/her rights to the leave or to put you on notice of the need for leave. However, the employee does need to state a qualifying reason for the leave. See "What's a Qualifying Event?" on page 44 to help recognize the circumstances that trigger the designation.

You must designate the time as FMLA/CFRA within two business days, absent any extenuating circumstances.

Designating Leave as FMLA/CFRA after It Begins

If you learn that the leave is for an FMLA/CFRA purpose after leave begins, as when an employee gives notice of the need to extend his/her paid leave with unpaid FMLA/CFRA leave, you may count the entire — or some portion of — the paid leave retroactively as FMLA/CFRA.

> **Example:** An employee is granted two weeks paid vacation leave for a skiing trip. In mid-week of the second week, the employee contacts you for an extension of leave as unpaid leave, and advises you that at the beginning of the second week of paid vacation, he/she suffered a severe accident requiring hospitalization. You would notify the employee that you are designating both the extension and the second week of paid vacation leave (from the date of the injury) as FMLA/CFRA leave.

However, when the employee takes sick pay that turns into a serious health condition (e.g., bronchitis that turns into bronchial pneumonia), and the employee gives notice of the need for an extension of leave, you may designate the entire period of the health condition as FMLA/CFRA leave.

Designating Leave after the Employee's Return

After an employee returns from paid or unpaid leave, you can retroactively designate the leave as family medical leave under FMLA/CFRA if:

- You did not learn the reason for the absence until the employee's return (e.g., where the employee was absent only briefly). In this case, you must notify the employee within two business days that you are designating the leave as family medical leave; or

- You were not aware that the reason for leave was an FMLA/CFRA qualifying reason, and the employee requests, within two business days of returning to work, that the leave be counted as family medical leave. If the employee does not make this request within two business days of returning to work, he/she is not eligible for FMLA/CFRA protection for the absence.

FMLA/CFRA and Workers' Compensation

The employee who is absent because of a work-related illness or injury and who is eligible for FMLA/CFRA should also be notified that the absences related to the workers' compensation leave will also count as FMLA/CFRA leave. For more information on workers' compensation, see Chapter 5, "Workplace Injury and Illness."

Holidays

If a holiday falls within a week taken as family leave, the week is nevertheless counted toward the employee's family leave entitlement. However, if you temporarily cease business, and your employees do not report for work for one or more weeks, the weeks your activities have ceased do not count against the employee's leave entitlement.

Examples of this situation include:

- An employer closing the plant for retooling; and
- School closing for two weeks for the Christmas/New Year holiday or summer vacation.

What You Should Do

It is always your responsibility to designate leave, paid or unpaid, as PDL- and/or FMLA/CFRA-qualifying, based on information provided by the employee, and to give the employee notice of the designation of the leave. Intermittent leave or leave on a reduced schedule requires only one notice unless the circumstances change.

Base your FMLA/CFRA designation decision on information you receive from the employee or his/her spokesperson only. If you have insufficient information about the reason for an employee's use of paid leave, ask the employee or his/her spokesperson to ascertain whether the paid leave is potentially FMLA/CFRA-qualifying.

Once you know that your employee's leave is for an FMLA/CFRA reason, promptly notify the employee, within two business days, absent extenuating circumstances, that his/her leave is designated as paid FMLA/CFRA leave.

If a dispute arises between you and your employee as to whether the paid leave qualifies as FMLA/CFRA, resolve it through discussions between you and the employee. Always document such discussions and decisions.

Provide the employee the appropriate letter notifying him/her that the leave counts against the PDL, FMLA, and/or CFRA entitlement:

- *Employee Letter - PDL Only*;
- *Employee Letter - PDL/FMLA*;
- *Employee Letter - CFRA Leave Taken after FMLA/PDL*; or
- *Employee Letter - FMLA/CFRA*.

 You can find these forms on the CD included with this product.

Paying the Employee

This section explains your obligations, if any, to compensate the employee taking family medical leave. It also describes the various state and federal employee-paid insurance entitlements that your eligible employees can obtain.

The Law Explained

FMLA/CFRA is unpaid leave. This means that you are not obligated to compensate an employee taking FMLA/CFRA leave. There are, however, a number of ways that an employee can obtain compensation through state disability insurance (SDI) and paid family leave (PFL) benefits, sick pay, vacation, and PTO.

State Disability Insurance (SDI)

If your employee is taking FMLA/CFRA leave for his/her own serious injury or illness, he/she can receive SDI payments. SDI is an employee-funded insurance program, and most employees are eligible for payments if absent for a qualifying reason. There is a seven-day waiting period before benefit payments begin. For more information, see "State Disability Insurance Defined" in Chapter 6, page 102.

Paid Family Leave (PFL)

Employees who are absent to care for a family member or to bond with a child during the first year after the birth, adoption, or placement for foster care may be eligible for PFL benefits. Like SDI, PFL is also an employee-funded insurance program. Benefits are available to eligible employees if the absence began on or after July 1, 2004. There is a seven-day waiting period before benefits begin. For more information, see "Paid Family Leave Defined" in Chapter 6, page 107.

> Although PFL benefits are available to employees on CFRA leave to care for a domestic partner or a domestic partner's child, those reasons are not covered by FMLA. For a discussion of CFRA leave for a registered domestic partner, see "Domestic Partners and CFRA" on page 56.

Vacation, Sick Pay, and Paid Time Off (PTO)

You may require that employees use sick pay, vacation, or PTO while taking leave under FMLA/CFRA, unless the FMLA leave is also PDL. You may not require the use of vacation or PTO during PDL/FMLA leave.

You may require the employee to use up to two weeks vacation prior to receiving PFL benefits. The first week of vacation would also serve as the seven-day waiting period before benefits begin. You may require the employee to use other paid time off during the waiting period if:

- He/she has no vacation available;
- You have a policy that requires the use of paid time off before an employee takes unpaid time off; and
- The paid time off is applicable to the type of absence.

> **Example:** An employee wants time off to bond with a new child but has no vacation. If your policy allows the use of sick pay for any reason, you could require the use of sick pay during the waiting period before PFL benefits begin. You could also require that the employee use sick pay to supplement the partial wage replacement provided by PFL benefits. However, if your policy prohibits the use of sick pay for any reason other than an employee's own illness/injury or kin care, you cannot require the employee to use sick pay. The employee is not ill, nor is the child — the employee is taking time for baby bonding.

The use of vacation, sick pay, or PTO during the seven-day waiting period will not impact SDI or PFL benefits. Once the employee begins SDI or PFL benefits, you may require, or the employee may choose, to supplement the benefit payment with accrued sick pay. However, the employee cannot receive total benefits in excess of his/

her usual wages. You should contact your local Employment Development Department (EDD) office to discuss supplementing SDI or PFL benefits with sick pay.

The following timeline shows SDI and PFL benefits during PDL, FMLA, and CFRA. The illustration shows the maximum 17 weeks for PDL and the maximum of 12 weeks for FMLA and for CFRA.

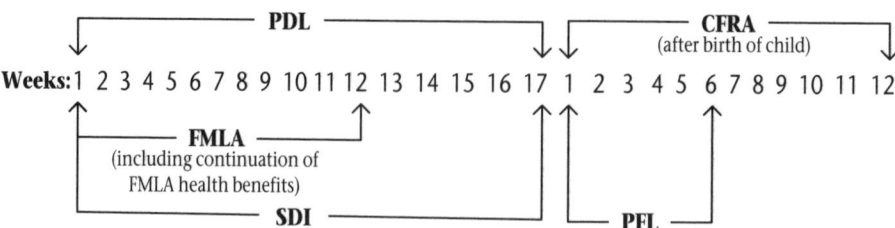

- An eligible employee may collect SDI for the duration of the time she is disabled by pregnancy, childbirth, or related medical condition after the initial seven-day waiting period for benefits to begin;

- If the employee receives SDI benefits (after the initial seven-day waiting period), there is no additional seven-day waiting period before PFL benefits begin;

- An eligible employee may collect PFL benefits for a maximum of six weeks in a 12-month period to bond with a new child;

- During PDL/FMLA, you may require the use of paid sick pay and permit the use of paid vacation. The use of paid sick leave will impact the amount of SDI benefits, but the use of paid vacation will not; and

- FMLA/CFRA requires that eligible employees be provided with continuation of health benefits as if the employee were still at work and on the payroll. Employees get one 12-week period of continued health benefits in each 12-month period. The leave does not have to be taken concurrently to retain health benefits.

Continuing Benefits

FMLA/CFRA law treats some benefits differently than others; in particular, it requires continuation of health benefits during the period of leave. To help keep things straight, this section covers the following benefits categories:

- Seniority, or employee status;

- Group health plan benefits, such as health, dental, and vision;

- Other insurance benefits, such as life, disability, and accidental death and dismemberment (ADD); and

- Retirement plans, such as 401k or pension plans.

The Law Explained

Employees on FMLA/CFRA leave (paid or unpaid) are entitled to retain employee status during the leave period. The leave does not constitute a break in service for purposes of longevity or seniority under any collective bargaining agreement or under any employee benefit plan.

The employee on FMLA/CFRA leave (paid or unpaid) is entitled to continuation of health benefits at the same level he/she had before the leave began. Health benefits include group health, dental and vision benefits. You may, however, require that employees continue to pay the portion of benefits that they would pay had they not taken FMLA/CFRA.

> **Example:** Your employee has health coverage for himself, for which you pay 90 percent and he pays 10 percent, deducted from his wages at the rate of $10 per week. The employee takes FMLA/CFRA leave for a total of eight weeks to care for his parent. For the duration of eight weeks of FMLA/CFRA leave, you must continue his health benefits as if he were still at work. You can require him to pay his portion —$10 per week for the eight weeks he is away on leave.

FMLA/CFRA leave periods (paid or unpaid) do not count as a break in service with regard to pension and other retirement plans for purposes of vesting and eligibility to participate. Unpaid FMLA/CFRA leave periods do not need to be treated as credited service for purposes of benefit accrual, vesting, and eligibility to participate. You must treat the employee on unpaid FMLA/CFRA as you do employees on other unpaid leave. If a plan requires an employee to be employed on a specific date in order to be credited with a year of service for vesting, contributions, or participation purposes, the employee on unpaid FMLA/CFRA leave on that date is deemed to have been employed on that date.

If your policy allows seniority to accrue when employees are on paid leave, such as paid vacation or sick leave, then seniority will accrue during any part of a paid FMLA/CFRA leave, consistent with your policy. If your policy allows seniority to accrue when employees are on unpaid leave, then seniority will accrue during any part of an unpaid FMLA/CFRA leave, again, consistent with your policy.

What You Should Do

1. The employee's seniority should not be less than what he/she had before FMLA/CFRA leave began:

    - If the FMLA/CFRA leave was unpaid, treat the accrual of seniority the same as you do other types of unpaid leave; and

    - If the FMLA/CFRA leave was paid (compensated with sick pay, vacation or PTO), treat seniority accrual the same as you do when employees take other types of paid leave.

2. If your policy states that employees earn vacation and sick pay at a specific rate for every hour that they work, or when they take paid sick or vacation leave, continue the accruals accordingly. Thus, the employee who uses paid vacation or sick leave would be accruing more vacation or sick leave, even when the paid leave is for FMLA/CFRA.

3. Continue the employee's health care coverage (if he/she has any) at the same level during the FMLA/CFRA leave, and offer COBRA coverage if the leave period expires.

4. Once the employee returns to work, make any payroll deductions to cover the employee's portion of the benefit as you normally would.

5. Use the appropriate FMLA/CFRA notice and include any amounts the employee must pay for benefits and the dates the payments are due.

Handling the Employee's Return to Work

When you grant an employee's family leave request, you must guarantee to reinstate the employee to the same or comparable position. Put the guarantee in writing if the employee requests. Only under very limited circumstances can you refuse to honor the guarantee of reinstatement.

> You should always consult with legal counsel before terminating, laying off, or refusing to reinstate an employee who is using family medical leave.

If you and your employee agree on a definite date of reinstatement at the beginning of the leave, you must reinstate the employee by or on that date. If the reinstatement date differs from your original agreement with the employee, you must reinstate the employee within two business days after the employee notifies you of his/her readiness to return.

The Law Explained

The employee returning from FMLA/CFRA must be reinstated with no less seniority than he/she had when the FMLA/CFRA leave began. This includes seniority for the purposes of layoff, recall, promotion, job assignment and seniority-related benefits such as vacation.

Employment in a "comparable position" means employment in a position that is virtually identical to the employee's original position in terms of:

- Pay;
- Benefits; and
- Working conditions, including:
  - Privileges;
  - Fringe benefits; and
  - Status.

The comparable position must involve the same or substantially similar duties and responsibilities, and should require substantially equivalent skill, effort, responsibility, and authority. The position must be performed at the same worksite, or one that is geographically close to the employee's previous worksite. Additionally, it means the same, or an equivalent shift or work schedule.

 An employee who returns from FMLA/CFRA leave, and for his/her own reasons, asks to return to a different job or a different schedule, is not entitled to any special consideration. Your obligation is to return him/her to the position he/she held prior to her leave. However, you should treat the employee's request the same as that of any other employee request for a change in hours or position.

Refusing to Reinstate a "Key" Employee

FMLA permits you to refuse reinstatement to a "key" employee if:

- The employee requesting the leave is a salaried employee;
- The employee requesting the leave is among the highest paid 10% of your workforce within 75 miles of his/her worksite;
- The refusal to reinstate the employee is necessary because the employee's reinstatement will cause your operations substantial and grievous economic injury; and

- You notify the employee of your intent to refuse reinstatement when you determine the refusal is necessary due to economic injury.

If the leave has already begun, you must give the "key" employee reasonable opportunity to return to work, following your notice to him/her that you intend to deny reinstatement.

> If you plan to deny reinstatement on this basis, it is strongly recommended that you seek the advice of legal counsel before taking such action.

Terminating Employees on FMLA/CFRA Before Leave Expires

As with other types of legally mandated leaves of absence, the employee on FMLA/CFRA leave has no greater right to reemployment than he/she would have, had they not taken the FMLA/CFRA leave.

When your employee is released to return to work, he/she returns to the job held before his/her leave, unless no longer able to perform that job. If an employee is unable to return to work after FMLA/CFRA, and the reason is their own disability, you may have to consider an extension of leave as a form of reasonable accommodation for the disability. For more information, see Chapter 4, "Disability Leave."

If the employee's inability to return is for a reason other than his/her own disability, you are obligated to provide additional leave only if your policy permits such leave. For more information, see Chapter 10, "Other Optional Leaves."

An employee returning from FMLA/CFRA is entitled to reinstatement to the same or equal position that he/she held before starting leave. It is unlawful to refuse reinstatement under the following circumstances:

- You distributed the employees job duties to several other employees and found that they could handle the additional workload;
- You hired a temporary employee as a substitute for your employee on FMLA/CFRA, and found that the temporary employee does a better job;
- You had to lay-off one person from a department, and selected the employee on FMLA/CFRA because he/she was already out of the workplace; or
- You have heard, through other employees, or even the employee on FMLA/CFRA, that he/she was considering not returning to work at the end of the leave.

Employee Layoffs

You can justify refusing to reinstate an employee if you can prove that you would have laid off the employee regardless of whether he/she was on FMLA/CFRA. This may be difficult to prove, unless you have documented proof that you would have laid off the employee based on:

- Seniority (for example, everyone with less than four years seniority was laid off);
- Position (for example, everyone in this same job was laid off);
- Department (for example, everyone in this department was laid off); or
- Other non-discriminatory factor (such as documented performance issues).

Termination for Other Reasons

Employees who abuse the leave of absence may be subject to disciplinary action, up to and including discharge. For instance, if an employee requests five days of FMLA/CFRA to care for a parent who is recovering from surgery, you would expect that the employee is doing just that. If the employee is seen engaging in other activities that would preclude him/her from caring for the ill parent, you may have a reason to terminate the employee.

However, if the employee requested FMLA/CFRA leave to care for a child in the hospital, and was actually caring for other children at home while his/her spouse was at the hospital with the ill child, you would probably not have sufficient reason to terminate the employee. The fact that the employee is entitled to leave and could have cared for the ill child in the hospital is enough to provide the employee protection under FMLA.

What You Should Do

1. Review the PDL and family medical leave policies in your employee handbook on an annual basis.

   Include in your policies information on any required payments for continuation of health benefits, and required use of sick pay (PDL/FMLA) or vacation (FMLA/CFRA).

2. Manage the employee's return using the *Certification of Physician or Practitioner for Employee Return to Work*, described in Table 8 on page 36.

3. Resume benefits upon the employee's reinstatement in the same manner and at the same levels as provided when the leave began, without any new qualification period, physical exam, or other requirement.

Forms and Checklists

New for 2005 The following table describes forms associated with family medical leave.

 You can find these forms on the CD included with this product.

Table 10. Forms and Checklists

Form name	What do I use it for?	When do I use it?	Who fills it out?	Where does it go?
Employee Letter - FMLA/CFRA	To notify the employee of the type of leave that has been granted.	At the beginning of the leave.	You do.	Send to the employee. Keep a copy in the employee's confidential medical file, separate from his/her personnel file.
Family/Medical Leave Policy (50 or More Employees)	To inform employees about their rights and responsibilities under state and federal family medical leave laws.	At time of hire and whenever you update the policy.	No filling out needed; you develop your policy based on this sample.	In your employee handbook; if you don't have a handbook, give a copy to every employee.
Federal Family and Medical Leave Act Poster (English)	To inform employees about their rights and benefits. Required if you have 50 or more employees.	At al times.	No filling out needed.	Display in a conspicuous location visible to all employees.

Table 10. Forms and Checklists *(continued)*

Form name	What do I use it for?	When do I use it?	Who fills it out?	Where does it go?
Federal Family and Medical Leave Act Poster (Spanish) **New for 2005**	To inform Spanish-speaking employees of their rights and benefits. Required if you have 50 or more employees.	At all times.	No filling out needed.	Display in a conspicuous location visible to all employees.
FMLA/CFRA Checklist for Employer Compliance	To help you comply with FMLA/CFRA.	When an employee: • Requests FMLA/CFRA leave; or • Is absent for an FMLA/CFRA qualifying reason.	You do.	In a file for all FMLA/CFRA leaves or in the employee's personnel file.
Medical Certification - FMLA/CFRA	To obtain physician or medical practitioner certification of the employee's need for leave.	When the employee requests FMLA/CFRA leave.	Patient's physician or medical practitioner. (The patient may be the employee or a a family member.)	In the employee's confidential medical file, separate from his/her personnel file.

Further Information

You can get more information about family medical leave from the following resources:

Table 11. Further Information

For information on	See these resources
PDL and CFRA	DFEH website at **http://www.dfeh.ca.gov/**.
FMLA regulations	U.S. Department of Labor (DOL) website at **http://www.dol.gov/dol/allcfr/ESA/Title_29/Part_825/toc.htm**. The DOL also provides a comparison of federal versus state family and medical leave laws at **http://www.dol.gov/esa/programs/whd/state/fmla/ca.htm**.
CFRA and PDL regulations	California Code of Regulations website at **http://ccr.oal.ca.gov**. Click the California Code of Regulations infobase link, then run a search for Title 2, Section 7297.0. To locate specific PDL regulations, run a search for Title 2, Section 7291.2.

Chapter 4
Disability Leave

State and federal disability laws require covered employers to reasonably accommodate the disability of any individual, if the employer knows of the disability, unless the employer can demonstrate that the accommodation would impose an undue hardship.

Reasonable accommodation includes:

- Reassignment to a vacant position;
- Part-time or modified work schedules; or
- An unpaid extension of a paid or unpaid leave.

 The forms mentioned in this chapter are on the CD included with this product.

The following table provides a broad overview of disability leave:

Table 12. Disability Leave

Disability leave issue	Requirement
Covered employers	State disability discrimination laws apply if you employ 5 or more employees. Federal law (the Americans with Disabilities Act [ADA]) applies if you employ 15 or more employees. See "Who's Covered?" on page 75.
Maximum amount of leave	You do not have to provide paid leave beyond that which is given to similarly-situated employees. You must make a reasonable accommodation to the known physical or mental limitations of a qualified applicant or employee with a disability unless it can show that the accommodation would cause an undue hardship on the operation of its business. See "Controlling Disability Leave" on page 78.

Table 12. Disability Leave *(continued)*

Disability leave issue	Requirement
Employee eligibility	An employee who is disabled and can perform the essential functions of his/her job is eligible. See "What is a Disability?" on page 72.
Reasons for leave	The disabled employee needs modified work or a period of leave for reasons related to their disability. See "Handling Employee Requests" on page 76.
Requirements for paid leave	You should allow an employee with a disability to exhaust paid leave first and then provide unpaid leave. The employee who is disabled may be entitled to State Disability Insurance (SDI). See "Paying the Employee" on page 79.
Employer responsibilities	When you learn that an employee has a disability that may require reasonable accommodation, engage in the interactive process to determine a reasonable accommodation. See "Handling Employee Requests" on page 76.
Ending the employment relationship before the leave expires	The employee has no greater rights than he/she would have if he/she were not disabled. The right to reinstatement would end if the employment relationship ends. However, you should consult with legal counsel before terminating an employee who is disabled. See "Handling the Employee's Return to Work" on page 81.
Interaction with other leaves	See "Controlling Disability Leave" on page 78.

What is a Disability?

Disability discrimination law protects qualified individuals with disabilities from disparate treatment by employers.

Disabilities come in all varieties. A person is considered disabled if he/she:

- Has a physical or mental impairment that limits one or more of the major life activities;
- Has a record of such an impairment;
- Is regarded as having such an impairment;
- Is regarded by the employer as having some condition that has no present disabling effect but may become a physical disability; or
- Has any health impairment that requires special education or related services.

Major life activities include caring for oneself, sleeping, learning, walking, interacting with others, working, and other physical, mental, and social activities.

California law has broader scope than federal law. The federal definition of disability requires that an individual be "substantially limited" in a major life activity. The California definition only requires the individual be "limited."

Excluded from Disabilities

Physical and mental disabilities do not include:

- Sexual behavior disorders;
- Compulsive gambling;
- Kleptomania;
- Pyromania;
- Psychoactive substance use disorders resulting from the current unlawful use of controlled substances or other drugs; and
- Homosexuality and bisexuality.

Who is a Qualified Individual?

A qualified individual with a disability is a person who meets legitimate skill, experience, education, or other requirements, and can perform the essential functions of the position with or without reasonable accommodation. An individual is not unqualified simply because he or she is unable to perform marginal or incidental job functions.

Essential Functions

You do not have to alter the essential functions of a job — that is not reasonable accommodation.

 Essential functions are fundamental job duties of the position or the reason the job exists.

You need to establish the essential functions of a job, both to determine whether an individual with a disability (with or without reasonable accommodation) is able to perform the job, and as a defense against any subsequent claim of discrimination. When determining essential functions:

- Document all important job functions;
- Be accurate and realistic;
- Stay current;
- Be flexible; and
- Review job descriptions with the employee in that job.

You are not required to reasonably accommodate a qualified individual with a disability if you can prove that the accommodation would cause undue hardship. The federal Equal Employment Opportunity Commission (EEOC) and the state Fair Employment and Housing Commission (FEHC) determine undue hardship on a case-by-case basis, taking into consideration the size of your business and the availability of tax incentives and assistance from the government.

The concept of **undue hardship** includes any accommodation that is unduly costly, extensive, or substantial, or an accommodation that would fundamentally alter the nature of the operation of your business.

You do not need to hire or retain a person who poses a direct threat to the health and safety of coworkers. The risk must be current, not speculative, not remote, not lessened by accommodation, and based on reasonable medical judgment or other objective evidence.

Reasonable Accommodation

A **reasonable accommodation** is any modification or adjustment in a job, an employment practice, or the work environment that allows a qualified individual with a disability to enjoy an equal employment opportunity.

The reasonable accommodation obligation is an ongoing duty, and may arise anytime a person's disability or job changes. You must engage in a timely, good faith, interactive process to determine and provide effective reasonable accommodations. You should document this process.

Disability Leave Defined

Disability leave provides a leave of absence as a form of reasonable accommodation for employees with a qualifying disability.

Who's Covered?

State disability discrimination laws apply if you employ five or more employees.

What's a Qualifying Event?

For purposes of this book, a qualifying event is a perceived or actual disability that limits the employee's ability to work, but that might be reasonably accommodated by some period of absence from work.

California law[6] requires that employers with 25 or more employees reasonably accommodate an employee who voluntarily enters and participates in alcohol or drug rehabilitation. For more information on this type of leave, see "Reasonable Accommodation for Rehabilitation" in Chapter 9, page 141.

Required Posters and Notices

Employers of five or more employees must post state and federal posters informing employees of their rights under state law — the Fair Employment and Housing Act (FEHA) — federal law, and the Americans with Disabilities Act (ADA). The *Equal Employment Opportunity is the Law* poster and *Discrimination and Harassment in Employment are Prohibited by Law (DFEH-162)* are available in the California Chamber of Commerce's all-in-one **Employer Poster**. For more information, contact customer service at (800) 331-8877 or visit **http://www.calchamberstore.com**.

What You Should Do

1. Review your employee handbook on an annual basis and include the appropriate policies. These may include:

   - *Equal Employment Opportunity Policy (5 or More Employees)*, described in Table 13 on page 82;

---

6. Cal. Lab. Code sec. 1025

- *Coordination of PDL with Family/Medical Leave Policy (50 or More Employees)*, described in Table 8 on page 37; and

- *Family/Medical Leave Policy (50 or More Employees)*, described in Table 10 on page 68.

Make note of any required payments for continuation of health benefits, and required use of sick pay or vacation (FMLA/CFRA and disability leave) in your employee handbook policies.

2. Provide the appropriate notices to the employee on disability leave. The law requires these two notices, both of which are included in the California Chamber's **Required Notices Kit**:

- *State Disability Insurance Provisions (DE 2515)*; and

- *For Your Benefit, California's Program for the Unemployed (Form 2320)*.

3. Post the required postings, including:

- *Equal Employment Opportunity is the Law* from the federal EEOC;

- *Discrimination and Harassment in Employment are Prohibited by Law (DFEH-162)*; and

- *Pregnancy Disability Leave Poster*, described in Table 8 on page 40.

Handling Employee Requests

California law requires you to provide reasonable accommodation to an employee who is disabled, if the accommodation helps the employee perform the essential functions of his/her job. Additionally, you must engage in a timely, good faith interactive process with the employee who needs reasonable accommodation.

If the disability is not apparent, the employee must provide you with sufficient information about the need for disability leave as an accommodation.

The Law Explained

You should respond quickly to a request for leave as a reasonable accommodation. If you and your employee with a disability need to engage in an interactive process, this should also proceed as quickly as possible. You should also act promptly to provide the reasonable accommodation. Unnecessary delays may result in a violation of state and federal disability laws.

Employee Responsibilities

If the disability is not apparent, the employee must provide at least verbal notice sufficient to make you aware of his/her need for reasonable accommodation in the form of disability leave.

Obtaining Medical Certification

To establish that an employee does have a disability and that reasonable accommodation in the form of some period of absence from work is required, you can require medical certification. However, you are not entitled to any medical diagnosis or any more information than necessary to determine that a disability exists, and what type or amount of leave your employee may need.

Designating Leave as FMLA/CFRA

If you have 50 or more employees and the employee is eligible, you should designate any time off for the illness or injury/disability of the employee as FMLA/CFRA, if appropriate. For more information, see Chapter 3, "Family Medical Leave," and the *Employee Letter - FMLA/CFRA*, described in Table 10 on page 68.

What You Should Do

1. You and your disabled employee should engage in an informal process to clarify what he/she needs and identify the appropriate reasonable accommodation. You may ask relevant questions to the individual that will enable you to make an informed decision about the request. This includes asking what type of reasonable accommodation is needed.

    The exact nature of the dialogue will vary. In many instances, the disability will be obvious, and thus there may be little or no need to engage in any discussion. In other situations, you may need to ask questions concerning the nature of the disability and the individual's functional limitations in order to identify the length of time needed as an accommodation.

2. Request medical certification from the employee, but only if you require it for other types of disability leave. You can use the *Medical Certification - FMLA/CFRA*, described in Table 10 on page 69, for this purpose.

3. Send the employee an *Employee Letter - FMLA/CFRA* (if the employee is eligible).

4. Complete a *Notice to Employee as to Change in Relationship*, described in Table 8 on page 38, to document the employee's leave of absence at the time the leave begins.

 You can find these forms on the CD included with this product.

Controlling Disability Leave

There is very little definitive legal guidance for the length of time you are "required" to provide disability leave time off. Each situation is unique and depends on the employee's own circumstances, the essential functions of the job, and whether the accommodation would cause you undue hardship.

If you have over 50 employees and the employee is eligible, you can designate the leave as FMLA/CFRA, for up to the maximum of 12 weeks in a 12-month period.

The Law Explained

While an extension of paid or unpaid leave is a form of reasonable accommodation for a disability, the question often arises, is it reasonable?

Reasonable accommodation is defined as any appropriate measure that allows an employee with a disability to perform the essential functions of his/her job. A modified or reduced work schedule, as well as time off from work, are examples of reasonable accommodation.

 There is no legal definition of "reasonable," but the law does allow an employer to refuse accommodation where it would be an undue hardship to the operation of the employer's business.

To deny accommodation on the basis of undue hardship, you must show that the accommodation requires significant difficulty or expense, when considered in light of:

- The nature and cost of the accommodation needed;
- The overall financial resources of the facilities involved, the number of persons employed at the facility, and how the operation of the facility would be impacted by the accommodation;
- Your overall financial resources, the overall size of the business (total number of employees), and the number, type and locations of all facilities;

- The type of operations, including the composition, structure, and functions of your workforce; and

- The geographic separateness or administrative or fiscal relationship of the facility or facilities.

Example: An employee needs an extended leave of absence for treatment for a disability. A small employer with only six employees would be more likely to suffer undue hardship than an employer who has hundreds of employees who perform the same job as the person needing the accommodation.

What You Should Do

There is no black and white legal guidance for reasonable accommodation. What works for one employer in terms of a reduced work schedule, leave of absence, or other accommodation may not be feasible for another. You should review each request for leave as reasonable accommodation for a disability and base your determination on the specific circumstances.

At some point, you may not be able to continue offering a leave with the guarantee of reinstatement, because the absence causes an undue hardship. You should consult with legal counsel before taking steps to terminate the employee. You might wish to consider continuing the leave, but without guaranteed reinstatement rights.

Paying the Employee

This section covers the types of payment an employee may be entitled to while taking leave as reasonable accommodation for a disability.

The Law Explained

Disability leave as reasonable accommodation, in itself, is not paid leave. However, disability leave might combine with other forms of leave or benefits, providing compensation for your employee.

State Disability Insurance (SDI)

Employees who need leave as a form of reasonable accommodation may be eligible for SDI compensation. SDI is an employee-paid insurance and virtually all employees are covered. For more information, see "SDI Qualifying Events" in Chapter 6, page 103.

Workers' Compensation

If the employee is disabled as a result of a work-related illness or injury, he/she is eligible for workers' compensation payments. For more information, see Chapter 5, "Workplace Injury and Illness."

Vacation, Sick Pay, and Paid Time Off (PTO)

You may require your employee to use paid time off, including vacation, sick pay, or PTO during any period of disability. If you require the use of paid time off, you should include the requirement in your employee handbook. For more information, see Chapter 8, "Vacation and Paid Time Off."

Continuing Benefits

If you have over 50 employees and the leave qualifies as FMLA/CFRA, continue to provide benefits at the same level you provided before the employee took the leave. This includes coverage for:

- Medical;
- Dental;
- Vision;
- Mental health;
- Coverage for the employee's dependents; and
- Other coverage you provide.

If you have fewer than 50 employees, the employee is not eligible for FMLA/CFRA, or the employee has exhausted his/her FMLA/CFRA leave, follow your own policy or practice with regard to continuation of benefits.

Your employee may be entitled to a Cal-COBRA or COBRA notice if he/she is not eligible for continuation of health benefits under FMLA/CFRA or your policy, or has exhausted all entitlements to continuation of benefits. Check your plan documents to confirm the length of time disabled employees remain covered by your health plan.

Handling the Employee's Return to Work

This section covers laws and tasks associated with returning the disabled employee to work.

The Law Explained

Generally, you must reinstate the employee to the job he/she held before using leave. If holding the position open would create an undue hardship, you must consider the employee for a vacant, equivalent position for which he/she is qualified. Transfer the employee to the vacant position for the duration of the leave and then reinstate him/her to that position when the need for leave ends.

If the employee can no longer perform the essential functions of his/her job, reasonable accommodation might include transfer to a different job or schedule. You may require medical certification of the need for accommodation.

You may also require that the employee obtain a release to return to work from his/her health care provider stating that he/she is able to resume work. You can use the *Certification of Physician or Practitioner for Employee Return to Work*, described in Table 8 on page 36, for this purpose. However, require a release only if you apply this practice uniformly or have a policy of requiring such releases from other employees returning to work after illness, injury, or disability.

Refusing Reinstatement

If you believe that an employee will pose a threat to his/her own safety or the safety of others, consult legal counsel before taking any action to terminate the employee. Although you may refuse to reinstate an employee on these grounds, you need to use caution.

Forms and Checklists

New for 2005 The following table describes forms associated with disability leave.

 You can find this form on the CD included with this product.

Table 13. Forms and Checklists

Form name	What do I use it for?	When do I use it?	Who fills it out?	Where does it go?
Equal Employment Opportunity Policy (5 or More Employees)	To inform employees that you comply with state and federal laws regarding equal employment opportunity, and how employees should report a claim of discrimination.	At time of hire and whenever you update the policy.	No filling out needed; you develop your policy based on this sample.	In your employee handbook; if you don't have a handbook, give a copy to every employee.

Further Information

You can get more information about disability leave from the following resources:

Table 14. Further Information

For information on	See these resources
Discrimination	• Equal Employment Opportunity Commission 901 Market Street, Suite 500 San Francisco, CA 94103 (415) 356-5100; • EEOC Compliance Manual, "Threshold Issues" section, at *http://www.eeoc.gov/policy/docs/threshold.html*; • Department of Fair Employment and Housing 2014 T Street, Suite 210 Sacramento, CA 95814 (916) 227-2873 or (800) 884-1684 *http://www.dfeh.ca.gov*; and • Fair Employment and Housing Commission 1390 Market Street, Suite 410 San Francisco, CA 94102 (415) 557-2325.

Chapter 5
Workplace Injury and Illness

Workers' compensation laws in California are complex and demanding. While this chapter gives you information on workers compensation in relation to time off, it is not meant to serve as a complete guide to workers' compensation. For a comprehensive guide to workers compensation, please refer to ***Workers' Compensation in California***, published by the California Chamber of Chamber of Commerce.

 The forms mentioned in this chapter are on the CD included with this product.

The following table provides a broad overview of workers' compensation:

Table 15. Workers' Compensation

Workers' compensation issue	Requirement
Covered employers	All employers are covered by workers' compensation law.
Maximum amount of leave	There is no legal maximum.
Employee eligibility	Generally, employees who suffer a work related injury are eligible for workers' compensation.
Reasons for leave	An illness or injury that results from a work-related cause. For more information, see "Who's Eligible?" on page 86.
Requirements for paid leave	Workers' compensation payments are made to employees who are injured as a result of work. If the employee is not able to return to work within three days of an injury or illness, he/she is entitled to temporary disability benefits. An employee using workers' compensation may also receive other types of compensation, including sick pay, vacation or paid time off (PTO). For more information, see Chapter 8, "Vacation and Paid Time Off."

Table 15. Workers' Compensation *(continued)*

Workers' compensation issue	Requirement
Interaction with other leaves, payments, and benefits	If you have 50 or more employees, and your employee is eligible, a disability that is covered by workers' compensation should run concurrently with FMLA/CFRA.
Employer responsibilities	You must post notices and provide pamphlets to employees, provide medical treatment and claim forms to injured employees, and hold the employee's job while he/she is on workers' compensation disability.
Ending the employment relationship before leave expires	The employee has no greater right to reinstatement than he/she would if he/she were not on workers' compensation. The right to reinstatement ends if the employment relationship ends. However, employees are protected by law from retaliation and termination based on the filing of a workers' compensation claim. You should consult with legal counsel before terminating an employee on workers' compensation.

Workplace Injury and Illness Defined

Workers' compensation insurance is a no-fault insurance system. It is a trade-off that exchanges your limited absolute liability for work-related injuries and illnesses for your employees' common law right to sue you for damages.

 Limited absolute liability means that an employer is responsible to compensate for work-related injuries, but the extent of the liability has limitations.

> **Example:** Workers' compensation insurance pays for all covered injuries or illnesses, even if there is no finding of fault. However, the amount of money that can be recovered is restricted to the amount established by law.

Any reasonable doubt as to the applicability of workers' compensation is generally resolved in favor of coverage. This benefits employers by making workers' compensation the exclusive remedy for workplace injuries or illnesses. However, exceptions to this exclusivity exist, either by statute or court decision.

 Exclusive remedy means that an injured employee who is covered by workers' compensation cannot sue an employer for other types of liability.

Workers' compensation is unique. It is a type of leave, a type of payment, *and* provides protection to employees who are unable to work as a result of a work-related illness or injury. Employees who file a workers' compensation claim are also protected by law from discrimination or discharge for filing a claim.[7]

Covered Injuries

Workers' compensation covers the following types of injuries, regardless of whether first aid or surgery is required or if the injury is work-disabling, and even if no medical treatment is required:

- Specific physical injury;
- Cumulative physical injury;
- Specific mental injury; or
- Cumulative mental injury.

 An injury is **specific** if there is one incident or exposure in the workplace that causes a physical or mental injury. An injury is **cumulative** if there are repetitive traumatic activities in the workplace which, extended over a period of time, cause injury.

Stress-caused Injuries

In order to receive workers' compensation benefits for a work-related stress (psychiatric) injury, an employee must show that the work-related stress was "predominant as to all causes (of the injury) combined." This essentially means that more than half of the employee's stress must come from his/her work, rather than from problems with the employee's family, health, or other concerns.

To be considered a compensable injury the employee must show:

- Diagnosis as a mental disorder (this diagnosis must be based on accepted and published terminology and criteria of the American Psychiatric Association);
- Medical determination that the mental disorder causes a disability or requires medical treatment; and
- Proof that "actual events of employment were predominant as to all causes combined," except in situations involving psychiatric injury as a result of a significant violent act, where working conditions must account for at least 35% (determined by the employee's doctor) of the sources of causation.

---

7. Cal. Lab. Code sec. 132(a)

Who's Covered?

If you are an employer in California, you must have workers' compensation insurance even if you only have one employee.

Who's Eligible?

Employee coverage generally begins the instant the employee is on the job — there is no qualifying period. Eligible employees include every "natural person" in the employ of another in California. It is irrelevant whether the party works under an oral or written contract, an express or implied contract, an apprenticeship, or even an unlawful arrangement.

Eligibility also extends to:

- Aliens;
- Minors;
- Elected and paid public officials;
- Persons employed by the owner or occupant of a residential building, and
- Paid directors of quasi-public corporations.

Casual workers must be employed at least 52 hours and earn $100 or more during a 90-day calendar period before the injury in order to be covered.

 Casual workers perform intermittent service on an as needed basis.

> ***Example:*** A retail establishment might have an employee who floats among departments as needed, or a preschool might bring in an additional teacher for a week to make sure state teacher/child ratios are met during attendance peaks, but the teacher isn't on staff all the time.

Who's Not Eligible

The Labor Code specifically excludes workers who are:

- Volunteers for a public agency or a private, non-profit organization and certain recreational camps, except certain public safety personnel;

- Deputy clerks, sheriffs, or constables appointed for their own convenience without compensation;

- Ski lift operators participating in recreational activities and uncompensated ski patrol;

- Participants in sports/athletics without compensation, students in amateur sporting events; and certain sports officials at non-professional events;

- Persons performing services in return for aid from religious, charitable, or relief organizations;

- Certain out-of-state law enforcement personnel deputized to work or acting as peace officers in California; and

- Independent contractors.

Required Posters and Notices

The law requires you to provide your employees with written notice regarding their workers' compensation rights. You must display or give to your employees:

- A workplace posting describing workers' rights if injured on the job;

- An employee pamphlet describing workers' compensation benefits and how to obtain them; and

- A notice for crime victims (when an employee is injured as the result of a crime).

If you have Spanish-speaking employees, you must post the notice in English and Spanish.

You must have workers' compensation insurance coverage and keep a copy of your certificate of insurance at every worksite.

Employee Pamphlet

You must give all new employees a workers' compensation pamphlet to inform them of their rights and obligations regarding workers' compensation. This pamphlet is in addition to the required poster discussed in the previous section.

If you have Spanish-speaking employees, you must provide the pamphlet in English and Spanish.

Written Notice for Crime Victims

If an employee is a victim of a workplace crime, you must give that employee written notice that he/she is eligible for workers' compensation benefits for resulting injuries, including psychiatric injuries. Provide a written notice either personally or by First Class mail within one day of the crime, or within one day of the date that you could have reasonably known of the crime.

Penalties for Failing to Post Notice

Failure to provide the required workers' compensation posting automatically permits the employee to be treated by his/her own physician for an injury occurring during the period in which the notice was not posted. Failure to post this notice may also be considered evidence of non-insurance. The California Chamber of Commerce produces a **Required Notices Kit** which contains all the required employer postings and pamphlets, including the DWC–approved workers' compensation poster. To order a **Required Notices Kit**, call (800) 331-8877 or visit our online store at *http://www.calchamberstore.com*.

The content of the workers' compensation poster and pamphlet changed as a result of legislation enacted in 2004. Be sure that your poster and pamphlet are current.

What You Should Do

Workers' compensation insurance is a requirement for all employers. The consequences of not having coverage will jeopardize your ability to continue your business. You should:

1. Make sure that your workers' compensation coverage is current.

2. Keep a certificate of coverage available at all worksites.

3. Place the required poster at all of your locations.

4. Give all new hires the required pamphlet.

Handling Employee Requests

Employees do not need to actually "request" workers' compensation; they are entitled to it by law should they become injured or ill as a result of work, regardless of whether they ask for it by name.

You should, however, require your employees to report all work-related illnesses or injuries to you immediately.

! You may discipline employees who fail to notify you of a workplace injury. You may also discipline employees who fail to follow your established safety policy, or who fail to follow the medical treatment plan established by the health care providers treating their workers' compensation illnesses or injuries.

! If you have 50 or more employees, and have an FMLA/CFRA eligible employee who has a workers' compensation claim, you should immediately send him/her written notice that any absences related to the workers' compensation injury will count towards his/her FMLA/CFRA entitlement. For more information, see Chapter 3, "Family Medical Leave."

The Law Explained

When an employee is injured as a result of a work-related incident, you must respond within specific timeframes. Several different California laws require these specific responses, including workers' compensation, Cal/OSHA, and employment laws.

What You Should Do

The major steps you must take in response to a reported illness or injury are:

1. Provide immediate medical care. You are required by law to provide emergency medical care for all work-related injuries.

   New for 2005 As of January 1, 2005, if you offer a medical provider network (MPN), you retain control of an injured employee's medical care indefinitely.

   If you do not offer an MPN, after 30 days of employer control of medical care, an employee can choose to be treated by a doctor of his/her own choice, if the doctor or clinic is within a reasonable geographic area.

   If you do not offer an MPN and the employee wishes to predesignate his/her own physician for workers' compensation treatment, the employee may do so only if:

   - The employee has notified you of the choice of his/her own physician, in writing and before the date of injury;
   - You provide non-occupational group health care coverage in a health services plan;

- The physician is the employee's primary care physician or surgeon holding an M.D. or D.O. (osteopathic medicine) degree and licensed under the Business and Professions Code;

- The physician has previously directed the treatment of the employee and controls the employee's medical records and medical history; and

- The physician agrees to be predesignated as the employee's treating physician for occupational injury or illness.

2. Should an incident result in a serious injury or death, you must report it within eight hours by telephone or fax to Cal/OSHA. (A web form is available online at ***http://www.dir.ca.gov/DOSH/WebComplaintForm.pdf***.)

   We recommend that you report it by both means. A serious injury is one that will require hospitalization of an employee for more than 24 hours, causes the loss or serious disfigurement of a body part, or causes death.

   You can find the location of the nearest Cal/OSHA office:

   - Listed in the government section of your phone book under state government agencies;

   - On the poster that you must display in your workplace (see "Required Posters and Notices" on page 87); or

   - Online at ***http://www.dir.ca.gov/dosh/DistrictOffices.htm***.

3. Notify the employee's emergency contacts, if the employee is unable to do so.

4. Provide the employee with the *Employee's Claim for Workers' Compensation Benefits (DWC 1)*, described in Table 16 on page 96, if the illness or injury will result in lost time beyond the date of the illness or injury, or results in medical treatment beyond first aid.

5. Prepare employer reports.

   You are required to file an *Employer's Report of Occupational Injury or Illness (Form 5020)*, described in Table 16 on page 97, within five working days (seven calendar days) after learning or being notified of any occupational injury or illness to any employee which results in lost time beyond the date of the injury or illness or which requires medical treatment beyond first aid.

   File the form with your workers' compensation carrier as soon as possible (within five days), or if you are self-insured, file the form with the Division of Labor Statistics and Research within five working days.

   If you have filed the *Employer's Report of Occupational Injury or Illness (Form 5020)* and the employee subsequently dies as a result of the illness or injury, you must send an amended report within five working days of learning of the death.

When an employee dies as a result of a workers' compensation illness or injury, you must file a *Notice of Employee Death (DIA 510)*, described in Table 16 on page 98, with the Division of Workers' Compensation (DWC), unless you have actual knowledge that the employee left a surviving minor child.

6. Communicate with the employee on a regular basis to make sure that he/she is receiving medical treatment and the required benefit payments in a timely manner.

7. Review the *Doctor's First Report of Occupational Injury or Illness*, described in Table 16 on page 96. The treating physician must complete this report and provide it to you and your workers' compensation carrier within five days of the physician's initial treatment/exam of the injured employee. You will want to note:

- The employee's written description of how the injury/illness occurred, in order to investigate the claim and/or the reason for the injury or illness;

- Whether or not treatment went beyond first aid. If it did, you must provide the employee with *Employee's Claim for Workers' Compensation Benefits (DWC 1)*, and you must complete the *Employer's Report of Occupational Injury or Illness (Form 5020)* and file both forms with your insurance carrier; and

- The employee's ability to return to his/her regular job or modified duty. A return to full duty or modified duty will reduce the payments made to the employee by the workers' compensation carrier and thus reduce the impact on your future insurance premiums.

8. Investigate the accident, identifying the cause and preventative action(s) that will avoid recurrence. Your Cal/OSHA mandated Injury and Illness Prevention Program requires that you investigate each accident. Be sure to document the investigation.

9. Prepare any required Cal/OSHA records, such as:

- *Injury and Illness Incident Report (Form 301)*;

- *Log of Work-Related Injuries and Illnesses (Form 300)*; and

- *Summary of Work-Related Injuries and Illnesses (Form 300A)*.

Use the *Guidelines for Determining OSHA Log 300 Recordability* to determine what you need to record. The *Optional Worksheet to Help You Fill Out the Annual Summary (Form 300A)* can help you complete *Form 300A*. For more information on these forms, see Table 16 on page 96.

You can find these forms on the CD included with this product. For help determining if you must record workplace injuries or illnesses on the Cal/OSHA log 300 forms, visit *http://www.hrcalifornia.com/log300*.

Controlling Workers' Compensation

While many of the laws that apply to workers' compensation are beyond the scope of this book, the basic requirements are listed below. For more detailed information, see ***Workers' Compensation in California***.

The Law Explained

There is no legally mandated maximum time period or limit on workers' compensation. Rather, the amount of time an employee is out on workers' compensation leave depends upon the extent of his/her injury and the determination of his/her health care provider regarding fitness to return to work.

There are limits on the amount of money the injured worker receives, based on his/her usual wages. It is in your best interest to get the injured employee back to work as soon as possible. Your workers' compensation insurance rates are based in part on the number of workers' compensation claims, and the amount of money paid to injured employees.

What You Should Do

1. Include in your written policy or employee handbook the requirement to promptly report any work-related illness or injury, and state that failure to report may result in disciplinary action, up to and including discharge.

2. Include in your written policy or employee handbook any requirements or other provisions for use of paid leave or time off during workers' compensation disability, and any requirement to use sick pay for doctor's appointments after the initial treatment. The sample *Workers' Compensation Policy*, described in Table 16 on page 98, contains sections covering these other provisions.

3. When appropriate, designate any time off from work for workers' compensation disability as FMLA/CFRA.

4. To retain more control of medical care, consider contracting with an approved MPN or Health Care Organization (HCO).

   If you do not have an MPN or HCO, select a company physician or clinic carefully. The individual or clinic you choose should be your partner in controlling costs and returning employees to work as soon as possible.

5. Consider using a pharmacy benefits manager to control costs. Prescription drugs are a large component of workers' compensation costs.

6. Work closely with your claims representative and/or case manager.

7. Investigate questionable claims.

8. Develop a temporary modified duty program.

9. Promote prompt closure of claims.

Paying the Employee

As the employer, you are not responsible for paying the employee directly for workers' compensation. You pay your workers' compensation insurance premiums, and your workers' compensation provider pays the employee. However, employees often believe they are entitled to more than one type of compensation.

You must pay for the employee's time during the first treatment by a health care provider for a workers' compensation illness or injury. After the initial treatment, the employee is under the control of the health care provider, and you are not required to pay for treatment-related absences from work. You may require that the employee use, or the employee may elect to use, paid time off, such as sick pay, for further doctor's appointments or physical therapy.

State Disability Insurance (SDI)

Employees cannot receive workers' compensation *and* SDI unless the workers' compensation rate is less than the SDI rate. If the workers' compensation rate is less than the SDI rate, the employee would receive the difference between the two rates as SDI, but would not receive a combined total of the two benefits.

Paid Family Leave (PFL)

Because PFL cannot be used for an employee's own illness or injury, an employee may not use PFL and workers' compensation concurrently.

Vacation, Sick Pay, and Paid Time Off (PTO)

Employees may receive payments for vacation, sick leave, or PTO without impacting their eligibility for workers' compensation payments.

You may require your employees to use vacation, sick pay, and PTO during any type of disability leave, including workers' compensation. If you do, you should have a written policy that requires your employees to use paid leave before taking unpaid or partially unpaid leave.

 If the employee is eligible for FMLA/CFRA, you may require him/her to use paid time off during a leave that runs concurrently with the workers' compensation disability.

Continuing Benefits

If you have 50 or more employees, and the employee is eligible for FMLA/CFRA, your employee maintains his/her health benefits for up to 12 weeks at the same level as if he/she were still at work.

If you have fewer than 50 employees, or the leave has expired, you may terminate the employee's health benefits and send a COBRA notice if:

- Your health plan is ERISA qualified; and
- You have exceeded the benefits provided for you by your contractual agreement with your carrier.

If your plan is not ERISA qualified, there is no law that states that you must continue health insurance benefits. However, there are cases[8] from the Workers' Compensation Appeals Board that indicate you must continue benefits as if the employee were still on the payroll. If you plan to terminate non-ERISA qualified health benefits for an employee on workers' compensation, consult with your legal counsel first.

---

8. *Navarro v. A&A Farming*, 67 Cal. Comp. Cases 296 (2002)

ERISA, the Employee Retirement Income Security Act, is the federal law concerning an employer's duties in administering an employee benefit program. ERISA is a comprehensive and important federal law relating to employee benefit plans. ERISA is a voluminous, technical piece of legislation that deals with establishing, operating and administering two types of employee benefit plans: welfare plans and pension plans.

What You Should Do

1. If your employee health plan is ERISA qualified, advise employees in your written policy or employee handbook the length of time coverage remains in effect for any type of illness or injury. The sample *Leaves of Absence Policy*, described in Table 16 on page 97, contains optional language you can use for this purpose.

2. Send a timely notice to the employee concerning Cal-COBRA/COBRA rights after the continuation of health benefits expire. For information on COBRA and the forms that may be necessary, see "COBRA and Cal-COBRA" in Chapter 1, page 12.

Handling the Employee's Return to Work

In most cases, the employee will be released to return to his/her job by the employee's health care provider. Once the employee has been released, you should reinstate him/her to the position he/she held before the injury.

However, an employee has no greater right to reinstatement to the same position than if he/she was continuously employed and not been out on workers' compensation.

The Law Explained

You can justify a refusal to reinstate the employee to his/her same position or duties if the employee is no longer able to perform the essential functions of the job or doing so would pose a serious threat to the safety of the employee or other employees.

You may place the employee on workers' compensation on layoff status if the decision to lay off the individual is based on a factor such as seniority, job classification, department, or other non-discriminatory factor used to determine layoffs. You should send the notice of the layoff to the employee on workers' compensation leave when you send notice to other employees.

What You Should Do

1. Keep your written job descriptions current. This will help the health care provider determine if an employee is fit for duty or modified duty.

2. Return disabled employees to work if the health care provider certifies the employee as able to perform essential functions of his/her job.

3. Offer vocational rehabilitation if needed.

Forms and Checklists

New for 2005 The following table describes forms associated with workplace injury and illness.

 You can find these forms on the CD included with this product.

Table 16. Forms and Checklists

Form name	What do I use it for?	When do I use it?	Who fills it out?	Where does it go?
Doctor's First Report of Occupational Injury or Illness	To review the results of an initial treatment.	After an injured employee's first doctor's visit.	The doctor.	In the employee's confidential medical file, separate from his/her personnel file.
Employee's Claim for Workers' Compensation Benefits (DWC 1)	To provide initial documentation of a workers' compensation claim, if the employee requires more than first aid.	Within 24 hours of notification of an employee injury.	The injured employee and you.	In the employee's file with the original insurer.

Table 16. Forms and Checklists *(continued)*

Form name	What do I use it for?	When do I use it?	Who fills it out?	Where does it go?
Employer's Report of Occupational Injury or Illness (Form 5020)	To report an employee's injury or illness, if the employee requires more than first aid.	Within five days following notice of injury or illness.	You do.	To your insurer or, if you are self-insured, to the Division of Labor Statistics and Research. Keep a copy in the employee's confidential medical file, separate from his/her personnel file.
Guidelines for Determining OSHA Log 300 Recordability **New for 2005**	To help you determine whether you need to record a work-related injury or illness on Log 300 forms.	When a work-related injury or illness occurs.	No filling out needed.	In your safety files, for your reference.
Injury and Illness Incident Report (Form 301)	To record a work-related injury or illness that qualifies as a recordable incident under Log 300 regulations.	When a recordable incident occurs.	You do.	In your safety files, for five years after the end of the year that the report covers.
Leaves of Absence Policy	To inform employees about how your company handles non-specific leaves of absence.	At time of hire and whenever you update the policy.	No filling out needed; you develop your policy based on this sample.	In your employee handbook; if you don't have a handbook, give a copy to every employee.
Log of Work-Related Injuries and Illnesses (Form 300)	To record all work-related injuries or illnesses that qualify as recordable incidents under Log 300 regulations.	Throughout any year in which you are required to maintain this log.	You do.	In your safety files, for five years after the end of the year that the log covers.

Table 16. Forms and Checklists *(continued)*

Form name	What do I use it for?	When do I use it?	Who fills it out?	Where does it go?
Notice of Employee Death (DIA 510)	To report an employee death.	At the time of an employee death for any reason, unless you know that the employee has a surviving minor child.	You do.	To the DWC.
Optional Worksheet to Help You Fill Out the Annual Summary (Form 300A) **New for 2005**	To gather the data needed to prepare *Form 300A*.	January of each year.	You do.	Discard after posting *Form 300A*.
Summary of Work-Related Injuries and Illnesses (Form 300A) **New for 2005**	To summarize the work-related injuries or illnesses that occur at a specific establishment during a year.	At the end of each year during which you must complete *Form 300*.	You do.	Post during February–April following the year that the summary covers. Keep in your safety files for five years after the end of the year that the summary covers.
Workers' Compensation Policy	To inform employees about how your company handles workers' compensation.	At time of hire and whenever you update the policy.	No filling out needed; you develop your policy based on this sample.	In your employee handbook; if you don't have a handbook, give a copy to every employee.

Further Information

You can get more information about workers' compensation and workplace safety from the following resources:

Table 17. Further Information

For information on	See these resources
Workers' compensation	• From the California Chamber of Commerce: ***Workers' Compensation in California***. • Division of Workers' Compensation at ***http://www.dir.ca.gov/DWC/dwc_home_page.htm***; • Commission on Health and Safety and Workers' Compensation at ***http://www.dir.ca.gov/CHSWC/chswc.html***; and • Workers' Compensation Appeals Board at ***http://www.dir.ca.gov/WCAB/wcab.htm***.
Safety	• From the California Chamber of Commerce: The ***Cal/OSHA Poster***, part of the ***Employer Poster*** available at ***http://www.calchamberstore.com***, lists contact information for various Cal/OSHA offices; • California Department of Industrial Relations at ***http://www.dir.ca.gov***; • California Division of Occupational Safety and Health at ***http://www.dir.ca.gov/DOSH/dosh1.html***; • California's Occupational Safety and Health Standards Board at ***http://www.dir.ca.gov/oshsb/oshsb.html***; • Model Injury and Illness Prevention Program for High Hazard Employers at ***http://www.dir.ca.gov/dosh/dosh_publications/iiphihzemp.html***; • Cal/OSHA guidelines for Workplace Security at ***http://www.dir.ca.gov/dosh/dosh_publications/worksecurity.html***; • User's Guide to Cal/OSHA at ***http://www.dir.ca.gov/dosh/dosh%5Fpublications/osha%5Fuserguide.pdf***; and • OSHA's SIC manual at ***http://www.osha.gov/pls/imis/sic_manual.html***.

Chapter 6
SDI and PFL

State disability insurance (SDI) and paid family leave (PFL)[9] are types of benefit payments collected and administered by California's Employment Development Department (EDD). Both SDI and PFL are funded by employee taxes through payroll deductions. SDI and PFL do not constitute an entitlement to leave, but rather are types of benefit payments an employee may receive while unable to work due to a qualifying reason.

Eligible employees may receive benefits while on a mandated leave such as Pregnancy Disability Leave (PDL). Employees not eligible for mandated leaves such as PDL or FMLA/CFRA may still receive SDI or PFL benefits for qualified absences.

 The forms mentioned in this chapter are on the CD included with this product.

The following table provides a broad overview of SDI and PDL:

Table 18. SDI and PFL

SDI/PFL issue	Requirement
Covered employers	With few exceptions, all employers are subject to SDI and PFL, although the tax is paid by employees. Most employees pay into the SDI and PFL fund.
Maximum benefit amount	The SDI benefit maximum is 52 times the weekly benefit amount, or the total wages earned in the base period, whichever is less. PFL benefits are approximately 55% of the employee's earnings. The maximum time during which PFL benefits can be paid is 6 weeks in a 12-month period.

---

9. Enacted through Senate Bill 777 in 2003

Table 18. SDI and PFL *(continued)*

SDI/PFL issue	Requirement
Employee eligibility	SDI benefits are payable to employees who are disabled by a non-work-related illness or injury, including pregnancy, that prevents them from performing their customary work. See "Who's Covered?" on page 102. PFL benefits are payable to employees who must care for a family member. See "Who's Eligible?" on page 108.
Interaction with other leaves, payments, and benefits	SDI benefits may be paid during PDL, FMLA/CFRA, and disability leaves, in combination with paid vacation, PTO, and sick pay. See "SDI Benefits" on page 105. PFL benefits may be paid during FMLA/CFRA leave and kin care, in combination with paid vacation, PTO, and sick pay. See "PFL Benefits" on page 110.
Employer responsibilities	You must make deductions from payroll, file required reports with EDD, respond to EDD requests for information, post notices in the workplace, and provide employees with pamphlets required by law.
Ending the employment relationship before the benefit expires	SDI and PFL do not protect employees from termination. However, where the individual is protected by a leave law, do not take action to terminate the individual before consulting legal counsel.

State Disability Insurance Defined

SDI benefits provide a partial wage replacement for individuals who take time off from work because of their own non-work-related illness, injury, or disability. The SDI tax has been in place for many years. The PFL tax is a relatively new tax, for which witholding began January 1, 2004. California law requires most employees to contribute to both SDI and PFL in the form of a payroll tax on the employee's wages.

Who's Covered?

Most employees in California are subject to SDI tax, and are eligible for benefits.

Exceptions to SDI coverage include:

- Individuals who perform ministerial duties;
- School districts and local government personnel;

- State employees;
- Individuals who rely on prayer for healing; and
- Individuals performing domestic service.

SDI Qualifying Events

An employee disabled by a non-work-related illness or injury, including pregnancy, may be eligible for SDI payments. A "qualifying event" for purposes of disability insurance involves both the disability itself, as well as a set of conditions which must be met in order for the employee to be eligible for benefits.

There is a seven-day waiting period before disability benefits begin. During the waiting period, eligible employees must:

- Be unable to perform their regular or customary work;
- Have a loss of wages as a result of a non-work-related disability; and
- Be under the care and treatment of a physician or practitioner who certifies that the person is disabled.

Employees must also file a timely claim — within 49 days from the date he/she became disabled. He/she also must have been employed or actively looking for employment when the disability began.

Other eligibility requirements for SDI benefits include:

- Having a disability that extends beyond the seven day non-payable waiting period;
- Receipt of at least $300 in wages, subject to SDI taxes, during the 12-month base period of the claim;
- Submission to a reasonable medical exam, if required; and
- Filing of a certificate of disability signed by a duly authorized medical or religious practitioner.

EDD calculates weekly benefit amounts using a **base period**. This base period covers 12 months and is divided into 4 consecutive quarters of 3 months each. The base period includes the wages an individual was paid approximately 5 to 17 months before the disability claim began, as long as those wages were subject to the SDI tax. Therefore, the base period does not include wages paid just before the disability began.

The employee cannot receive SDI payments if he/she is:

- Receiving unemployment insurance payments;
- Receiving full wages;
- In legal custody as a result of a conviction or when confined by court order; or
- Receiving workers' compensation at a weekly rate equal to or greater than the SDI rate.

SDI payments made be made if the employee is unable to perform his/her customary work. An employee is disabled on any day in which he/she is:

- Certified disabled by his/her doctor;
- Ordered not to work by a written order from a state or local health officer because he/she is infected with, or suspected of being infected with, a communicable disease; or
- Being medically treated for acute alcoholism or acute drug-induced illness.

Required Posters and Notices

All employers must post or provide the following SDI notices:

- The EDD posting *Notice to Employees: Unemployment Insurance, State Disability Insurance, and Paid Family Leave (DE 1857A)*. A copy of the posting is included on the California Chamber's **Employer Poster**; and
- The EDD pamphlet, *State Disability Insurance Provisions (DE 2515)*. Give the pamphlet to each new employee within five working days of hire; and to each employee who becomes disabled due to pregnancy or who becomes ill, injured or hospitalized due to causes unrelated to work. You must provide the pamphlet within 10 days of notification that the employee's absence is the result of any of these occurrences. Copies of the pamphlet are included in the California Chamber's **Required Notices Kit**.

Medical Certification

Privacy law prevents you from requiring medical certification that gives a diagnosis or other medical information. If the employee is absent because of his/her own serious illness or injury, you may request a statement from the employee's health care provider stating that the employee is unable to work. The payment of SDI benefits is handled by EDD, which requires its own certification of eligibility.

The *Medical Certification - FMLA/CFRA* form, described in Table 10 on page 69, is an example of how such a medical certification might look.

For PFL purposes, you may require a written statement from an employee that confirms that the reason for his/her absence is one covered by PFL and/or kin care. The payment of PFL benefits is handled by EDD, which requires its own certification of eligibility.

 You can use the *Request for Use of Kin Care*, described in Table 21 on page 120, to obtain the employee confirmation.

SDI Benefits

New for 2005 Employees who meet all of the eligibility requirements may be paid for up to 52 weeks. The weekly benefit amount is based on the wages in the highest quarter of the employee's base period. The weekly benefits range from a minimum of $50 to a maximum of $840 (increased from 2004).

SDI and PDL

The usual disability period for a normal pregnancy is up to four weeks before the expected delivery date, and up to six weeks after the actual delivery date. The doctor may certify a longer period of disability if:

- The delivery is by Cesarean section;
- There are medical complications; or
- The employee is unable to perform her regular or customary job duties.

Employees who are eligible for PDL or PDL running concurrently with FMLA may receive SDI payments during the period of PDL disability. Once the employee is no longer disabled, both the FMLA/PDL leave and SDI benefits end. See "Paying the Employee" in Chapter 3, page 60 for a timeline showing the relationship of PDL and FMLA, as well as the time period for receiving SDI benefits. For more information on pregnancy disability, see Chapter 2, "Pregnancy Disability Leave."

SDI and Other Types of Disability

An employee who is absent for his/her own disability that is not related to pregnancy or a work-related illness or injury may also be eligible for FMLA/CFRA leave. FMLA/CFRA leave is an entitlement to up to 12 weeks of leave within a 12-month period. The employee who is eligible for SDI benefits could receive those benefits during the FMLA/CFRA leave, and up to an additional 40 weeks of SDI benefits beyond the right to the protected leave. The actual amount of time the employee can draw SDI benefits depends on his/her earnings in the base period before the disability began.

An employee who receives SDI benefits is not entitled to job protection. Absent some protection under another law (such as PDL, PDL/FMLA, FMLA/CFRA or reasonable accommodation for a disability), there is no guaranteed reinstatement simply because the employee receives SDI benefits.

For more information on family medical leave, see Chapter 3, "Family Medical Leave." For more information on disability leave, see Chapter 4, "Disability Leave."

SDI and Other Wages

Vacation is not considered a form of wages for the purpose of SDI benefits. You may require or you may allow employees to use vacation while they are receiving SDI benefits, or to supplement SDI benefits.

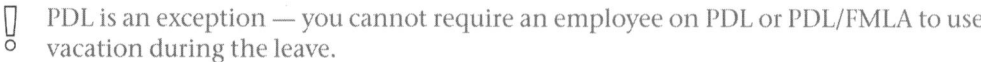

PDL is an exception — you cannot require an employee on PDL or PDL/FMLA to use vacation during the leave.

Paid sick leave and PTO are a form of wage replacement for SDI benefit purposes. An employee cannot receive more money than they would normally make if at work. You may require or allow an employee to use sick pay or PTO during the seven-day waiting period for SDI benefits to begin. Once the employee is receiving SDI benefits, you may require or allow him/her to use sick pay or PTO to supplement the SDI benefits. You should coordinate this type of payment with your local EDD office.

An employee who receives paid sick leave for kin care is not eligible for SDI benefits, as they are caring for someone else.

Paid Family Leave Defined

As of January 1, 2004, all employees subject to SDI tax began paying an additional tax to fund PFL benefits. PFL benefits became available for claim periods beginning on or after July 1, 2004.

PFL benefits are intended to provide a partial wage replacement for individuals who take time off work to care for a family member or bond with a new child.

This table shows the relationship among state and federal mandatory leave laws, and California's new PFL benefits:

Table 19. Paid Family Leave

Issue	FMLA, CFRA, PDL (state and federal law)	PFL (new state law)
Employer coverage	FMLA/CFRA — 50 or more employees at a worksite. PDL — 5 or more employees.	One or more employees.
Employee eligibility	FMLA/CFRA — Has worked for you for 12 months and 1,250 hours in the prior 12-month period. PDL — Immediate for a period of actual disability.	Immediately upon employment and need for leave. Requires seven-day waiting period (unless the employee already served the seven-day waiting period for SDI) and subject to your vacation policy.
Duration	FMLA/CFRA — 12 weeks in a 12-month period (leave is typically unpaid). PDL — Periods of actual disability, up to 4 months.	Six weeks in a 12-month period.
Reasons for leave	FMLA/CFRA — For the employee's own serious health condition; to care for a seriously ill child, parent, or spouse; or for baby bonding (bonding with a newborn child or a child placed with the employee in connection with adoption or foster care). PDL — Disability due to pregnancy or pregnancy-related conditions.	To care for a seriously ill family member (parent, spouse, child, or domestic partner) or for baby bonding. See "PFL Qualifying Events" on page 109.

Table 19. Paid Family Leave *(continued)*

Issue	FMLA, CFRA, PDL (state and federal law)	PFL (new state law)
Requirement for medical certification	Yes, you may require medical certification.	Yes. The EDD provides forms.
Vacation or PTO pay during leave	You may require the employee to use accrued vacation or PTO if leave is for a reason other than pregnancy disability.	You may require the employee to take up to two weeks of accrued vacation or PTO before becoming eligible for benefits.
Reinstatement rights	You must reinstate the employee to the job held prior to the need for leave.	Creates no reinstatement rights. The right may exist under some other law or company policy.
Continuation of benefits	The employee is entitled to the same level of benefits as if he/she were still on the payroll. The employee pays any contribution they would pay if they were at work.	No benefit continuation unless it exists under some other law.
Relationship to current leave laws	**New for 2005** FMLA/CFRA run concurrently unless the employee is disabled by pregnancy or the leave is to care for a registered domestic partner. If the employee is disabled by pregnancy, PDL runs concurrently with FMLA and the employee will be entitled to CFRA after she is no longer disabled by the pregnancy. An employee in a registered domestic partnership is not entitled to FMLA to care for his/her domestic partner, but is entitled to CFRA for that purpose.	PFL benefits are available to eligible employees who are on FMLA/CFRA leave to care for a seriously ill family member (parent, spouse, child, or domestic partner) or for baby bonding.

Who's Eligible?

Most employees in California who are subject to SDI tax will be subject to PFL tax and eligible for PFL benefits.

The exceptions to PFL tax are the same as those for SDI tax. For more information, see "Who's Covered?" on page 102.

Required Posters and Notices

EDD's most current version of *Notice to Employees: Unemployment Insurance, State Disability Insurance, and Paid Family Leave (DE 1857A)* contains the required information about PFL. EDD has also developed a *Paid Family Leave (DE 2511)* pamphlet, which must be given to all employees hired on or after January 1, 2004. Additionally, as of July 1, 2004, you must give this pamphlet to anyone taking a leave in order to care for an ill family member or to bond with a new child.

You can order copies of the PFL posting and pamphlet directly from EDD at **http://www.edd.ca.gov**. The California Chamber of Commerce also produces a **Required Notices Kit** which contains all required employer postings, including the EDD notices. To order a **Required Notices Kit**, call (800) 331-8877 or visit our online store at **http://www.calchamberstore.com**.

PFL Qualifying Events

In order to be eligible for PFL benefits, the employee must need leave in order to:

- Care for a seriously ill family member — a parent, spouse, child, or domestic partner; or
- Bond with the employee's new child, the new child of the employee's spouse or domestic partner, or a child in connection with the adoption or foster care placement of the child with the employee or the employee's spouse or domestic partner.

For more on domestic partners, see "California Domestic Partner Rights and Responsibilities Act" in Chapter 1, page 10, and "Domestic Partners and CFRA" in Chapter 3, page 56.

There is a seven-day waiting period before PFL benefits begin. Where a claim for PFL is filed following a pregnancy-related SDI claim, there is no second waiting period. Eligible employees must:

- Be covered by SDI or a voluntary plan in lieu of SDI and have earned at least $300 from which deductions were withheld;
- Complete all claim forms;
- Supply medical information to support their claim;

- Provide required documentation if leave is to bond with a new child; and
- Use up to two weeks of paid vacation if required by their employer.

An individual cannot receive PFL payments if he/she is:

- Receiving SDI benefits;
- Receiving unemployment or workers' compensation benefits;
- Not working or looking for work;
- Not suffering a loss of wages;
- Unable to prove that there is a need for care, through documentation by the ill individual's health care provider; or
- In custody as a result of conviction for a crime.

PFL Benefits

New for 2005 Employees who meet all of the eligibility requirements may be paid for up to six weeks in a 12-month period. The weekly benefit amount is based on the employee's wages in the highest quarter of the employee's base period. The weekly benefits range from a minimum of $50 to a maximum of $840 (increased from 2004).

The employee who is out for his/her own disability may receive SDI benefits while on a protected leave, such as PDL, PDL/FMLA, or FMLA/CFRA. PFL benefits are not paid during the time the employee is disabled. However, if the employee wishes to take time off for baby bonding or to care for a seriously ill parent, spouse, or child, he/she may receive PFL benefits during the time that is also designated FMLA/CFRA or CFRA.

Example: A pregnant employee is eligible for PDL/FMLA leave and SDI benefits for the time she is disabled — two weeks prior to the birth of her child and six weeks after. Her PDL/FMLA disability leave and her SDI benefits end when her pregnancy disability ends, as certified by her health care provider. If she chooses to take up to 12 weeks of CFRA leave for baby bonding, she will now use four weeks of FMLA/CFRA and eight weeks of CFRA. She may receive partial pay from PFL for the first six weeks of CFRA-only leave. The final six weeks of CFRA would be unpaid, unless she had other benefits available to her.

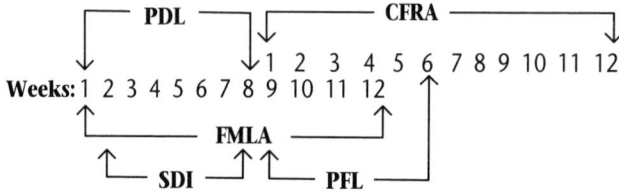

If an employee is taking up to 12 weeks of FMLA/CFRA to care for a seriously ill parent, spouse, or dependent child, the employee may be eligible for PFL benefits for up to six weeks in a 12-month period.

Example: An employee who is eligible for FMLA/CFRA needs 12 weeks to care for a seriously ill parent. He is required by his employer to use up to two weeks of unused vacation, and he does so, for the first two weeks of FMLA/CFRA. The next six weeks of FMLA/CFRA, he receives PFL benefits. Then, the last four weeks of FMLA/CFRA are unpaid, unless the employee has other benefits available to him.

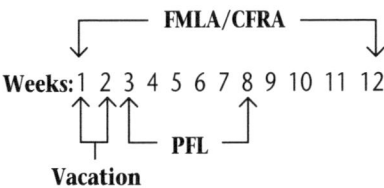

PFL and PDL

An employee who is disabled by pregnancy is eligible for SDI benefits, but not for PFL benefits. However, once she is no longer disabled by the pregnancy (and her SDI benefits cease), she may apply for PFL benefits during the time she takes off to bond with her new child.

PFL and Family Medical Leave

PFL benefits are payable only when an individual is caring for a family member or bonding with a new child. An eligible employee could receive PFL payments for a maximum of six weeks in a 12-month period while on FMLA/CFRA leave to:

- Care for a spouse, parent, dependent child, or domestic partner; or
- Bond with a new child of the employee, his/her spouse, or domestic partner; or one placed with the employee for adoption or foster care.

Note that while PFL benefits are available while an employee is on leave to care for a domestic partner or to bond with a child of his/her domestic partner, these situations do not qualify as FMLA leave. However, legislation passed in 2003 and effective in 2005 gives domestic partners the same legal rights as legal spouses, providing CFRA rights to domestic partners. For more on domestic partner rights, see "California Domestic Partner Rights and Responsibilities Act" in Chapter 1, page 10, and "Domestic Partners and CFRA" in Chapter 3, page 56.

PFL and Other Wages

You may require the use of up to two weeks of vacation when an employee applies for PFL benefits. The first week of vacation pay would be available for the seven-day waiting period before PFL benefits begin.

Since PFL benefits do not totally replace an employee's earnings, you may require or allow the use of paid sick leave, PTO, and/or vacation to supplement PFL payments. You may require the employee to use other paid time off to supplement PFL benefits if you have a policy that requires the use of other paid time off to supplement benefit payments such as SDI and workers' compensation, and the paid time off is applicable to this type of absence.

Under PFL law, the payment of other types of benefits does not impact the amount of the employee's PFL benefits.

> ***Example:*** An employee wants time off to bond with a new child and uses two weeks of vacation, as required by your policy, prior to receiving PFL benefits. The employee then receives partial wage replacement from PFL benefits. Your policy allows the use of sick pay for any reason, and you require the use of such paid time off to supplement PFL and SDI benefits. The employee would be required to use sick pay to supplement the PFL benefits.
>
> If your policy prohibits the use of sick pay for any reason other than the employee's illness, injury, or kin care, you may not require that the employee use sick pay to supplement PFL benefits, as the time off is for baby bonding, not illness.

Transfers, Benefits, and Reinstatement Rights

Employees who receive SDI or PFL payments have no protected rights — including no rights to transfers, continued employment, employee benefits, and reinstatement, unless the right exists by provision of some other law or your policy or practice.

The continuation of benefits does not exist simply because the employee is receiving SDI or PFL benefits. However, if the payment of SDI or PFL benefits is protected by PDL or FMLA/CFRA, the employee would continue to receive benefits at the same level as if he/she were at work.

What You Should Do

In order to comply with SDI and PFL law, you should:

1. Deduct SDI and PFL taxes from employees' wages according to the rates set by EDD.

2. Make appropriate payments and file reports with EDD.

3. Post *Notice to Employees: Unemployment Insurance, State Disability Insurance, and Paid Family Leave (DE 1857A)* in the workplace.

4. Provide new hires with the *State Disability Insurance Provisions (DE 2515)* and *Paid Family Leave (DE 2511)* pamphlets.

5. When an employee becomes disabled or is absent for a reason that would qualify for SDI/PFL benefits, provide the employee with the following pamphlets:

    - *State Disability Insurance Provisions (DE 2515)*;
    - *For Your Benefit, California's Program for the Unemployed (Form 2320)*; and
    - *Paid Family Leave (DE 2511)*.

6. When the leave of absence begins, send the employee the *Notice to Employee as to Change in Relationship*, described Table 8 on page 38.

7. Make sure your employee handbook includes any requirements for the use of vacation, sick pay, or PTO during an absence or leave of absence. This might include absences that are also PDL, PDL/FMLA, FMLA/CFRA, workers' compensation, disability as an accommodation, and kin care.

8. Implement a method of tracking employee absences and notifying employees in writing of the designation of leave as one or more of the above types of leave.

9. Notify employees when any leave has expired or been exhausted.

10. Consult with legal counsel before taking disciplinary action or terminating anyone on any protected leave or taking a mandated benefit.

Further Information

You can get more information about SDI and PFL from the following resources:

Table 20. Further Information

For information on	See these resources
SDI/PFL benefits, downloadable forms, etc.	EDD's website at **http://www.edd.ca.gov**.
Estimating weekly benefit amounts	EDD's *State Disability Insurance (SDI) and Paid Family Leave (PFL) Weekly Benefit Amounts* at **http://www.edd.cahwnet.gov/direp/de2588.pdf**.

Chapter 7
Sick Leave and Kin Care

This chapter covers sick leave and kin care as absences as well as types of payment. In particular, sick leave refers to a benefit that provides some amount of payment for employees taking time off because of illness.

The forms mentioned in this chapter are on the CD included with this product.

Sick Leave/Kin Care Defined

Sick pay provides employees with pay during leave taken for a short-term illness.

If you provide paid sick leave, you must allow employees to use up to one half of their yearly accrual for the purpose of caring for their ill child, parent, spouse or domestic partner. The use of sick leave for this purpose is known as kin care. You may not count time used as kin care against an employee in any absence control program, and employees are protected from discipline, discharge, demotion or suspension.[10]

Time off that may be used for a combination of vacation, sick leave, or another reason is usually referred to as paid time off (PTO). Employers typically offer vacation and sick leave as separate benefits, or offer PTO, which can be used at the employee's discretion. Because PTO may also be used for sick leave, one half of PTO may be used for kin care.

Because PTO may be used for kin care, references in this chapter to "sick leave" also refer to "PTO" unless noted otherwise.

Who's Covered?

There is no law requiring you to offer paid sick leave as a benefit; it is up to you. However, if you do not have a bona fide sick leave plan, you cannot deduct wages from

---
10. Enacted through Assembly Bill 1471 in 2002

an exempt employee's salary for complete days of absence for illness. If you deduct such wages, you jeopardize his/her exempt status. If the employee is non-exempt/hourly, you can deduct for any absences for sickness.

You determine the rate of accrual, or amount of sick days an employee may use.

What is a Qualifying Event?

Paid sick leave is a benefit that employees may use to replace wages if they are ill or injured, whether the absence is non-work or work related. You may, by policy, require the use of sick leave before the employee takes unpaid leave. You may require the use of sick leave for doctor's appointments and other types of treatment, including those that are for a work-related illness or injury.

If you offer paid sick leave benefits, California kin care law requires you to allow employees to use up to one half of their paid sick leave accrual to care for their ill child, parent, spouse, or domestic partner. For more information on domestic partners, see "California Domestic Partner Rights and Responsibilities Act" in Chapter 1, page 10.

Required Posters and Notices

While there are no legally required posters or notices, you should notify employees of any requirements to use paid sick leave before taking unpaid leave. This can be a part of your policy in your employee handbook. The sample *Sick Leave Policy*, described in Table 21 on page 120, provides language you can use.

Handling Employee Requests

If your employee is absent or requests time off for his/her own illness, or to care for a family member, what do you do?

The Law Explained

Your employees are responsible for notifying you of the need for sick leave. You may by policy require that employees provide medical certification of the need for leave and their ability to return to work (fitness for duty) if the leave is due to their own illness or injury.

What You Should Do

If the time off is also covered by a protected type of leave such as PDL, FMLA/CFRA, or kin care, be sure to let the employee know of any medical certification requirements or other documentation. If your policy requires medical certification for absences of a specified length, be sure to put that in the sick leave policy in your employee handbook.

Controlling Sick Leave and Kin Care

You may require medical certification if sick leave is for the employee's own illness or injury. You may also require medical certification clearing the employee's return to work. If the absence is to care for a family member, and the employee will be using kin care, you may require the employee to sign a statement saying that the time off is for kin care. You can use the *Request for Use of Kin Care*, described in Table 21 on page 120, for this purpose.

You should implement some method of tracking the accrual of paid sick leave, whether it accrues on a rate determined by your policy, or whether it is a set amount that an employee receives each year.

> **Example:** You could allow employees to accrue up to five days, or 40 hours per year. In this scenario, employees would accrue 3.33 hours per month. Or, at the beginning of each year, you could give each employee 40 hours of sick leave for the year.

You also need to track the use of paid sick leave to make sure you are not paying employees for time off that they do not have available. For accrual purposes, as well as payment at termination, PTO is treated the same as vacation. For more information, see Chapter 8, "Vacation and Paid Time Off."

If you overpay an employee, you cannot deduct the overpayment from his/her wages.

Paying the Employee

Paid sick leave typically replaces an employee's wages at the regular rate of pay. However, an employee's illness or injury may exceed the amount of sick leave he/she has accrued. There is no requirement that you continue to pay an employee who has used up all of his/her paid sick leave or kin care. There are, however, some exceptions to deducting from the salary of an exempt employee.

The Law Explained

An employee who needs time off may be eligible for SDI or PFL benefits in addition to paid sick leave. SDI or PFL benefits only partially subsidize an employee's regular rate of pay. You may require that employees receiving SDI or PFL benefits use paid sick leave (or other paid time off) to supplement the benefits and provide whole compensation, if you have a policy that requires the use of other paid time off to supplement benefit payments, and the paid time off is applicable to this type of absence.

> ***Example:*** Weekly SDI benefits are based on the highest quarter of earnings in the employee's base period. An employee who makes $10 an hour might have earned $5,200 in the highest quarter of earnings. The weekly benefit at that level is approximately $220. This employee normally earns $400 per week. He/she does not receive any other type of compensation to make up the loss of $180 per week. You may require or allow the employee to supplement the SDI benefit with 18 hours of sick leave (18 x $10 = $180) so that the employee continues to receive his/her regular earnings.

Employees who use kin care (half of their accrued sick leave) to care for a family member may also be eligible for PFL benefits (if the absence begins on or after July 1, 2004).

What You Should Do

If you require or allow the use of sick leave to supplement SDI or PFL benefits, you must coordinate the payments with EDD. If the employee receives other wages, such as sick leave, military pay, commissions, modified duty wages, bonuses, or holiday pay, he/she may lose SDI/PFL benefits.

You may coordinate kin care or other paid leave benefits with PFL so that the employee receives an amount equal to his/her regular wages. For more information on SDI and PFL, see Chapter 6, "SDI and PFL."

Continuing Benefits

Employees on paid leave usually continue benefit coverage as if they were at work. If the paid leave runs concurrently with FMLA/CFRA, you must continue the benefits as if the employee were on the payroll. For more information, see "Continuing Benefits" in Chapter 3, page 62.

If the employee has exhausted FMLA/CFRA leave or is not eligible, you should continue health benefit coverage in accordance with your policy or practice. Be sure to review your summary plan description — it defines how long benefits continue when an employee is disabled for any reason.

Once the employee exhausts his/her rights to health benefit coverage as noted above, you should send him/her a notice of Cal-COBRA or COBRA rights. For information on COBRA and the forms that may be necessary, see "COBRA and Cal-COBRA" in Chapter 1, page 12.

Handling the Employee's Return to Work

An employee who is using time off for sick leave or kin care does not have any greater right to reinstatement than he/she would if still at work. However, you may not count the time taken as kin care against the employee, including for the purpose of any absence control policy that you may have in place.

The Law Explained

Employees who use kin care, as well as other protected leaves (such as PDL and FMLA/CFRA) are protected against retaliation, discharge, and discipline for taking such leaves.

What You Should Do

If you offer paid sick leave as a benefit, you should include the following in your employee handbook or written policy:

- The accrual rate, any cap or limits on carryover, or forfeiture of unused sick leave;
- Restrictions on the use of sick leave, such as no accrual until after the employee has been with you for a specified period of time;
- Any requirements to take paid sick leave before taking unpaid leave. Be sure to list all types of absences to which this policy applies. This includes the required use of sick leave for any absences that are otherwise unpaid (including work-related and non-work-related illness or injury), or supplementing disability benefits, such as SDI and PFL;
- Requirements for a specific type of notice or form for identifying paid sick leave; and
- Any medical certification requirement.

Forms and Checklists

New for 2005 The following table describes forms associated with sick leave and kin care.

 You can find these forms on the CD included with this product.

Table 21. Forms and Checklists

Form name	What do I use it for?	When do I use it?	Who fills it out?	Where does it go?
Request for Use of Kin Care	To enable employees to request sick leave that qualifies as kin care.	When an employee requests time off to care for a family member.	Employee.	In the employee's confidential medical file, separate from his/her personnel file.
Sick Leave Policy	To inform employees about the sick leave you offer and requirements for its use.	At time of hire and whenever you update the policy.	No filling out needed; you develop your policy based on this sample.	In your employee handbook; if you don't have a handbook, give a copy to every employee.

Chapter 8
Vacation and Paid Time Off

You are not required by law to offer employee benefits such as vacation or paid time off (PTO). If you do offer such benefits, you may require your employee to use paid time off during absences that might otherwise be unpaid. This chapter guides you through the wage and hour issues relevant to vacation and PTO, as well as the various leaves during which you may require an employee to use these benefits.

 The forms mentioned in this chapter are on the CD included with this product.

Vacation and PTO Defined

Vacation and PTO are a type of benefit that you may choose to offer your employees. If you do offer this benefit, both vacation and PTO are considered to be a form of wages that employees earn as they work. Under California's wage and hour laws, vacation and PTO must accrue and must be paid out at termination. The only exception is where the benefit is provided through an Employee Retirement Income Security Act (ERISA) qualified plan.

Vacation is typically used by employees to pay for time away from work for their own personal use and enjoyment. PTO typically combines both sick leave and vacation allowances into one block of time. The employee can use PTO for personal reasons, vacation, or sick leave.

Employers who have a separate vacation policy generally have a sick leave policy as well. PTO usually combines traditional forms of sick leave and vacation into one comprehensive personal leave.

> **Example:** A sick employee might use two days of PTO during an illness, and then three weeks later use a week of PTO for a vacation.

Required Posters and Notices

There are no poster or notice requirements associated with vacation/PTO benefits.

Handling Employee Requests

You decide when an employee can use vacation or PTO, and whether an employee accrues additional vacation/PTO while taking vacation/PTO. You should document this policy in your employee handbook.

 You can find sample *Vacation Policy* and *Paid Time Off Policy* forms on the CD included with this product. For more information on these forms, see Table 22 on page 126.

Controlling Vacation and PTO

You generally pay an employee on vacation/PTO the same rate as you would for his/her regular duties. Employees can also use vacation/PTO with other forms of leave.

The Law Explained

The following subsections illustrate how California law requires the use of vacation or PTO during other types of leaves.

Using Vacation During PDL

Although you may not require the use of vacation or PTO during an absence that is also PDL, you must permit the use of vacation or PTO during PDL should the employee request the benefit during her pregnancy disability. The choice to use vacation/PTO is the employee's. The employee must, however, meet any eligibility requirements you set by your policy or practice in order to use vacation or PTO during an absence that is for PDL.

Using Vacation During FMLA/CFRA

You may require the use of vacation or PTO during all FMLA/CFRA absences that are not related to pregnancy disability. Be sure to mention any such requirements in your employee handbook policies.

Using Vacation During Sick Leave/Kin Care

You typically do not pay out two benefit types concurrently. However, you may have a policy that requires the use of any paid time off before the use of unpaid time. Employees may use PTO for any absence, including vacation or sick leave.

Vacation is not subject to the kin care law, but PTO is. PTO is a combination of vacation and sick leave. Unless you further define PTO, an employee could use all of his/her PTO for vacation or for sick leave. Since all of the time could be sick leave, employees can use up to one half of their yearly PTO accrual for the purpose of kin care.

Vacation and Disability Benefits

Although vacation and PTO are considered a form of wages under wage and hour law, they are treated differently under disability insurance law.

You may require or allow the use of vacation and PTO when an employee is receiving state benefits such as workers' compensation, SDI, and PFL. If you require the use of vacation or PTO, you should include such requirements in your employee handbook policy.

PFL regulations specifically state that you may require the use of up to two weeks of vacation when the employee applies for PFL. The first week of paid vacation would be in lieu of the unpaid week of waiting time. For more information on PFL, see "Paid Family Leave Defined" in Chapter 6, page 107.

The use of vacation while an employee is receiving SDI benefits does not reduce those benefits. However, PTO is treated the same as sick leave and its use *does* reduce SDI benefits. You may require or allow the use of PTO to supplement SDI benefits.

What You Should Do

1. Regularly reconcile an employee's vacation/PTO accruals with time he/she has taken. If you do not plan to advance vacation that has not yet been earned, notify the employee that he/she cannot take more vacation/PTO until it has accrued. You might want to send written notice, on a regular basis, advising employees of the amount of accrued time remaining for vacation/PTO.

2. Keep in mind that if you advance vacation or PTO, it is considered an employee debt and you cannot later deduct the money from the employee's wages, even if he/she has not accrued enough time off to "pay back" the advance.[11]

3. When preparing final paychecks for employees who are leaving your employ, or who have been laid off, you must pay out any accrued, unused vacation or PTO at the time of termination.

Paying the Employee

California law does not require that employers provide vacation or PTO. However, if you offer these benefits, you must follow specific rules.

The Law Explained

If you provide vacation or PTO benefits, there are several wage and hour rules that you must follow:

- Vacation and PTO are considered wages and must be earned and vested as the employee works;

    Example: If the accrual rate you set for vacation is two weeks/ten days per year, after six months the employee will have earned one week/five days of vacation.

- Vacation pay and PTO accrue as they are earned and cannot be forfeited, even when the employment relationship ends, regardless of the reason;

- Although you can place a reasonable cap on vacation/PTO accrual, you must give employees a reasonable amount of time to use up vacation/PTO before they stop accruing time;

- Accrued vacation/PTO is paid out at termination at the employee's final rate of pay, not at the rate in effect when the employee accrued the vacation/PTO;[12]

- You determine at what point the employee begins to earn vacation/PTO (for example, after the first month, three months, or six months of employment); and

- The accrual rate cannot decelerate — you cannot have an accrual rate of two weeks after six months of employment and two weeks after the following year — such a plan would be a deceleration of accrual — the employee earns no vacation during the first six months, accrues vacation at the rate of 1.66 days per month during the second six months of employment, and accrues 0.833 days per month during the second year.

---

11. 2002 update of the *DLSE Enforcement Policies and Interpretations Manual* sec. 11.2.5
12. Cal. Lab. Code sec. 227.3

> Employees may file a wage and hour claim with the state Labor Commissioner or in Superior Court if you fail to pay out accrued and unused vacation/PTO wages at termination. If the employee wins, he/she may collect a waiting penalty of one day's wage for every day (up to 30) that the wages were unpaid. The employee can go back in time up to four years for unpaid wages.
>
> However, if you have an illegal "use it or lose it" policy, there is no statute of limitations on such a claim.
>
> For additional information on wage and hour law, see the ***2005 California Labor Law Digest***.

Continuing Benefits

You must continue benefits for an employee on vacation/PTO as you would if he/she were actively working. However, you decide whether an employee continues to accrue vacation, PTO or sick leave while using vacation, PTO, or sick leave.

What You Should Do

Include the following in your employee handbook or written policies:

- The time period during which accrual begins for new hires, the rate of accrual, and any incremental increases in accrual, such as for more years of service;
- Any eligibility requirements, restrictions on the use of vacation or PTO and any required use, including during a leave of absence;
- Any requirements that vacation be requested in advance, in writing, or be approved by a supervisor or other individual; and
- The form or other documentation that is required for reporting time not worked as vacation or PTO.

Chapter 8: Vacation and Paid Time Off

Forms and Checklists

New for 2005 The following table describes forms associated with vacation and PTO.

 You can find this form on the CD included with this product.

Table 22. Forms and Checklists

Form name	What do I use it for?	When do I use it?	Who fills it out?	Where does it go?
Paid Time Off Policy	To inform employees about the PTO you offer and requirements for its use.	At time of hire and whenever you update the policy.	No filling out needed; you develop your policy based on this sample.	In your employee handbook; if you don't have a handbook, give a copy to every employee.
Vacation Policy	To inform employees about the vacation you offer and requirements for its use.	At time of hire and whenever you update the policy.	No filling out needed; you develop your policy based on this sample.	In your employee handbook; if you don't have a handbook, give a copy to every employee.

Chapter 9
Other Legally Protected Absences

This chapter covers other types of absences protected by state and federal laws. Below are the specific requirements of each type of absence, as well as any documentation that you may require, wage and hour issues, continuation of benefits, and return to work rights.

 The forms mentioned in this chapter are on the CD included with this product.

Military Service Leave

Employees may be called to, or volunteer for active duty in the military. They are entitled to time off to perform their duties.

The Law Explained

Employees who volunteer or are ordered to military service or training are protected by federal law with regard to re-employment and continuation of benefits.[13]

New for 2005 On December 10, 2004, President Bush signed the Veterans Benefits Improvement Act of 2004 (VBIA), providing reinstatement rights and other benefits for veterans and employees who are called for military duty. The new law has two important implications for employers:

- The period for continuation of health care coverage has been extended from 18 to 24 months; and

- You must post a new employee notice describing rights, benefits, and obligations under the Uniformed Services Employment and Reemployment Rights Act of 1994 (USERRA).

---
13. Uniformed Services Employment and Reemployment Rights Act of 1994, Public Law 103–353

The US Department of Labor (DOL) is developing the regulations for the new law. To learn about the regulatory requirements as they become available during 2005, subscribe to the Chamber's free e-mail newsletter, **Labor Law Extra**, at *http://www.laborlawextra.com*.

You can find additional information about your responsibilities and employees' rights under USERRA at:

- The DOL USERRA Advisor, at *http://www.dol.gov/elaws/userra0.htm*; and
- The National Committee for Employer Support of the Guard and Reserve (ESGR), at *http://www.esgr.com*.

Employee Protection

Protected military service includes:

- Active duty;
- Active duty for training;
- Initial active duty for training;
- Inactive duty training;
- Full-time National Guard duty; and
- Absences for examinations to determine fitness for duty.

The maximum length of leave time is five years. The five years of leave is cumulative of all absences from employment due to military service. There are exceptions to the five year limit:

- Time required to complete an initial period of obligated service;
- Time during which an individual was unable to obtain orders releasing him/her from service through no fault of his/her own; and
- Time required to fulfill additional training requirements determined by the military to be necessary for professional development or completion of skill training and retraining; or time during which an individual is ordered to remain on active duty under certain federal laws.

Documentation

You may require that an employee give advance notice of the need for leave when possible. Typically the employee receives military orders for when and where he/she is to report for duty or training. This should suffice as documentation of the need for leave.

You may require that the employee returning from military service leave provide documentation establishing that:

- The person's application is timely;
- The person has not exceeded the cumulative five years of service; and
- The person has not lost his entitlement to protection under federal law as the result of a dishonorable discharge or other factors.

Paying the Non-Exempt Employee

Non-exempt employees do not get paid for any time that they do not work. You may by policy or practice provide some paid time off for military service, but there is no legal requirement to do so.

You must allow the employee to use any accrued paid vacation, PTO, or similar paid time off, if the employee makes such a request.

Paying the Exempt Employee

Exempt employees are subject to both state and federal law and you may not deduct from the salary of an exempt employee unless the employee has performed no work during the workweek. The amount of time the employee works does not matter. The performance of any work during a workweek in which the employee is absent for military service requires payment of the employee's weekly salary.

You must allow the employee to use any accrued paid vacation, PTO, or similar paid time off, if the employee makes such a request.

Continuing Benefits

New for 2005 Federal law provides benefits similar to COBRA for the employee on military service leave. If the employee elects this coverage, he/she may continue coverage for up to 24 months while on military service (increased in 2004). You may not charge more than 102% of the full premium. However, if the employee's leave is for less than 31 days, you may not require that he/she pay more than the normal employee share of the cost of the health insurance. For information on COBRA and the forms that may be necessary, see "COBRA and Cal-COBRA" in Chapter 1, page 12.

Employees on military service leave do not incur a break in service for purposes of pension rights.

Employees returning from military service leave are entitled to all other rights and benefits they would have had if they had remained continuously employed.

Handling the Employee's Return to Work

Employees who take leave for military service are entitled to reinstatement as follows:

- Less than 90 days of service: The employee is entitled to reinstatement to the same position he/she would have had if there had been no military service. In other words, if the employee would have been promoted had he/she not been on military service leave, you must promote him/her, unless he/she is no longer qualified to perform that job. If the employee is no longer able to perform that job, you must make reasonable efforts to qualify him/her. If that is not possible, you must return the employee to the job he/she held at the time the military service leave started.

    Reasonable efforts to qualify the employee might include additional time for training or other remedial efforts to put the employee back to where they would have been, if not for the military service;

- 90 or more days of service: You must re-employ the employee to the position he/she would have had but for the military service, or a position of like seniority, status, and pay, if the employee is qualified to perform one of those jobs. If the employee is not qualified to perform one of those jobs, you must make reasonable efforts to qualify him/her. If the reasonable efforts fail, you must re-employ the person in the job he/she held at the time military service leave began, or a position of like seniority, status and pay; and

- If the employee returns with a military-related disability, you must reasonably accommodate him/her. Place the person in the position he/she would have held, if not for the military service. If performance of that job is impossible even with reasonable accommodation, you must provide a job of equivalent seniority, pay and status for which the person is qualified, or for which he/she could become qualified with reasonable effort.

    If neither of these options is feasible because of the disability, you must provide another position of lesser status and pay but with full seniority.

    If two or more individuals are entitled to the same position and report for work, the individual who left the position first has the right to that position.

You are not required to re-employ an individual returning from military service leave if:

- Your circumstances have changed to the extent that re-employment is impossible or unreasonable;

- Retraining or accommodating a disabled individual would pose an undue hardship for you; or

- The employment prior to the military service leave was for a brief, non-recurrent period with no reasonable expectation that the employment would continue indefinitely or for a significant period.

> **Example:** You would not be required to reinstate someone returning from military service leave if you have previously laid off all employees in a similar job, department, or with like seniority. If you have no positions the individual is able to perform (with or without reasonable accommodation for his/her disability), or the individual was employed for a short period of time as a part-time or temporary employee, with the understanding that the job was not long-term, then you are not required to reinstate the employee.

What You Should Do

1. Include in your employee handbook or written policy:

    - Any paid time off for military service leave;

    - Any requirements for documentation of service; and

    - Any requirements for using paid time off before taking unpaid time off.

   You cannot discriminate against someone for taking military service leave. Any requirements to use paid time off should apply to all types of leave.

   For appropriate language, see the sample *Military Leave Policy*, described in Table 23 on page 152.

New for 2005 2. Post the new USERRA notice, due to be published by the DOL in spring 2005. The California Chamber will make the new notice available as part of its **Required Notices Kit** as soon as it is finalized by the DOL. For more information, visit **http://www.calchamberstore.com**.

3. Require documentation of any required training or active duty.

4. Send notice to the employee that the time counts against his/her entitlement for military service.

5. Pay the employee for vacation, PTO, or other paid time off, if you require it or the employee requests it.

6. Continue the employee's health benefits (if any) and notify the employee of any required payments.

7. Pay the exempt employee for any week in which he/she performs any work.

8. Reinstate the employee as required by law.

9. Make sure that the employee returning from leave receives all benefits and rights as if he/she had been continuously employed.

Jury/Witness Duty Leave

Employees at certain times are requested to perform jury duty or appear as a witness in a trial. The absence from work for these reasons is protected by law, and you cannot deny the employee the time off.[14]

The Law Explained

All employers are subject to the laws that prohibit discrimination or retaliation against an employee who takes time off for jury duty or to appear as a witness.

All employees are considered to be protected when engaged in the following types of activities:

- To serve on an inquest jury or trial jury; and
- To appear in court in compliance with a subpoena or court order as a witness or where the individual is a victim of crime.

Your employees cannot be exempted from jury duty merely because it's something they don't want to do, it's inconvenient, or they are needed at work. You as the employer cannot get an employee excused from jury duty.

There is a provision for a one time postponement of jury service. An employee might ask for a postponement because of a planned vacation, business trip, or other conflict. This does not excuse the employee from jury service; it merely postpones it.

---

14. Cal. Lab. Code sec. 230

Documentation

You may require advance notice of the need for jury/witness duty, where it is reasonable to do so. If the employee is unable to give advance notice, you may not take any action against the employee if he/she can provide certification of the need for leave within a reasonable amount of time after the absence.

An employee who is called for jury duty will receive a summons from the court and can request proof of service from the jury clerk if he/she has to report for duty. The summons or proof of service from the court is sufficient certification.

Paying the Non-Exempt Employee

Non-exempt employees do not get paid for any time that they do not work. You may by policy or practice provide some paid time off for jury/witness duty, but there is no legal requirement to do so.

You must allow, and may require, employees to use any accrued vacation, PTO, or other paid time off available to the them.

Paying the Exempt Employee

Exempt employees are subject to both state and federal law and you may not deduct from the salary of an exempt employee unless the employee has performed no work during the workweek. The amount of time the employee works does not matter. The performance of any work during a workweek in which the employee takes jury/witness duty leave requires payment of the employee's weekly salary.

Continuing Benefits

You cannot discriminate against an employee who takes time off for jury/witness duty. Benefits should be handled the same as for employees who are absent for similar periods of time. If the employee is on paid leave, benefits typically continue at the same level as if the employee were at work.

Return to Work

You cannot discriminate against an employee who takes time off for jury/witness duty. Absent extenuating circumstances, such as layoffs or the employee's physical or mental inability to return to work, the employee must be reinstated to his/her job.

If you need to lay off an employee who is taking jury/witness duty leave, remember that the employee has the same rights and seniority as if he/she had been at work.

> If you need to terminate or lay off an employee who is taking this type of leave, consult legal counsel.

You can find more information about jury duty and your obligations as an employer at *http://www.courtinfo.ca.gov/jury/index.htm*.

What You Should Do

1. Include in your employee handbook or written policy:
   - Any paid time off for jury/witness duty;
   - Any requirements for documentation of service; and
   - Any requirements for using paid time off before taking unpaid time off.

> You cannot discriminate against someone for taking jury/witness duty leave. Any requirements to use paid time off should apply to all types of leave.

   For appropriate language, see the sample *Jury Duty and Witness Leave Policy*, described in Table 23 on page 152.

2. Require documentation of the need for leave.

3. Pay the employee for vacation, PTO, or other paid time off, if you require it or the employee requests it.

4. Continue the employee's health benefits (if any) and notify the employee of any required payments.

5. Pay the exempt employee for any week in which he/she performs any work.

6. Reinstate the employee as required by law.

7. Make sure that the employee returning from leave receives all benefits and rights as if he/she had been continuously employed.

Domestic Violence/Sexual Assault Victims Leave

Employees who are victims of domestic violence or sexual assault may need time off to appear in legal proceedings. Absence from work for this reason is protected by law and you cannot deny the employee the time off. If you have more than 25 employees, you must also allow the employee time off to seek various types of assistance related to the domestic violence/sexual assault.

The Law Explained

All employers are subject to the laws that prohibit discrimination or retaliation against an employee who takes time off due to being a victim of domestic violence or sexual assault.

You must allow an employee who is the subject of domestic violence/sexual assault time off to seek any relief (such as a restraining order or other injunctive relief) to ensure the health, safety, or welfare of the employee or his/her child.

If you have 25 or more employees, you must also allow the employee up to 12 weeks off in a 12-month period to do any of the following:

- Seek medical attention for injuries caused by domestic violence or sexual assault;
- Seek legal assistance or remedies related to the domestic violence or sexual assault;
- Obtain services from a domestic violence or sexual assault shelter or program, or rape crisis center;
- Obtain psychological counseling related to experiences of domestic violence or sexual assault;
- Participate in safety planning related to the domestic violence or sexual assault; or
- Take other actions to increase safety from future domestic violence, including temporary or permanent relocation.

Documentation

You may require advance notice of the need for this type of leave, where it is reasonable to do so. If the employee is unable to give advance notice, you may not take any action against the employee if he/she can provide certification of the need for leave within a reasonable amount of time after the absence.

Certification that is sufficient includes:

- A police report indicating that the employee was a victim of domestic violence or sexual assault;

- A court order protecting or separating the employee from the perpetrator of an act of domestic violence or sexual assault;
- Other evidence from the court or prosecuting attorney that the employee has appeared in court; or
- Documentation from a medical professional, domestic violence advocate or advocate for victims of sexual assault, health care provider, or counselor that the employee was undergoing treatment for physical or mental injuries or abuse as a result of domestic violence or sexual assault.

You must maintain the confidentiality of requests for or documentation of leave for domestic violence or sexual assault. Keep any medical certification in a separate, confidential medical file.

Paying the Non-Exempt Employee

Non-exempt employees do not get paid for any time that they do not work. There is no legal requirement that you pay non-exempt employees who need domestic violence/sexual assault leave.

You must allow, and may require, employees to use any accrued vacation, PTO, or other paid time off available to the them.

Paying the Exempt Employee

Exempt employees are subject to both state and federal law and you may not deduct from the salary of an exempt employee unless the employee has performed no work during the workday. The amount of time the employee works does not matter. The performance of any work during a workday in which the employee takes domestic violence/sexual assault leave requires payment of the employee's daily salary.

Continuing Benefits

You cannot discriminate against an employee who takes time off as a result of domestic violence or sexual assault. Benefits should be handled the same as for employees who are absent for similar periods of time. If the employee is on paid leave, benefits typically continue at the same level as if the employee were at work.

Return to Work

You cannot discriminate against an employee who takes time off as a result of domestic violence or sexual assault. Absent extenuating circumstances, such as layoffs or the employee's physical or mental inability to return to work, the employee must be reinstated to his/her job.

If you need to lay off an employee who is taking domestic violence/sexual assault leave, remember that the employee has the same rights and seniority as if he/she had been at work.

> If you need to terminate or lay off an employee who is taking this type of leave, consult legal counsel.

What You Should Do

1. Include in your employee handbook or written policy:

    - Any requirements for documentation of the need for leave; and
    - Any requirements for using paid time off before taking unpaid time off.

    > You cannot discriminate against someone for taking domestic violence/sexual assault leave. Any requirements to use paid time off should apply to all types of leave.

    For appropriate language, see the sample *Domestic Violence/Sexual Assault Victims Leave Policy (1-24 Employees)* and *Domestic Violence/Sexual Assault Victims Leave Policy (25 or More Employees)*, described in Table 23 on page 151.

2. Require documentation of the need for leave.

3. Send notice to the employee that the time counts against his/her entitlement for domestic violence/sexual assault leave.

4. Pay the employee for vacation, PTO, or other paid time off, if you require it or the employee requests it.

5. Continue the employee's health benefits (if any) and notify the employee of any required payments.

6. Pay the exempt employee for any day in which he/she performs any work.

7. Reinstate the employee as required by law.

8. Make sure that the employee returning from leave receives all benefits and rights as if he/she had been continuously employed.

Victims of Crime Leave

An employee who is a victim of a violent crime, or whose immediate family member is a victim, may take time off to attend judicial proceedings related to that crime.[15]

The Law Explained

All employers must grant leave for employees to attend judicial proceedings if they meet the eligibility requirements. There are no restrictions on the length of time. However, the time off from work must be in order to attend judicial proceedings related to the violent crime (a violent felony, serious felony, or a felony theft or embezzlement).

Employers may not discharge or discriminate against an employee who is absent to attend judicial proceedings related to a crime. This protection extends to compensation or other terms, conditions or privileges of employment, and includes protection of seniority.

Who's Eligible?

Eligible employees include any employee who is:

- The victim of a violent crime;
- An immediate family member of a victim;
- A registered domestic partner of a victim; or
- The child of a registered domestic partner of a victim.

For more information on domestic partners, see "California Domestic Partner Rights and Responsibilities Act" in Chapter 1, page 10.

Immediate family member includes the employee's:

- Spouse;
- Child or stepchild;

---

15. Cal. Lab. Code sec. 230.2

- Brother or stepbrother;
- Sister or stepsister;
- Mother or stepmother; and
- Father or stepfather.

Documentation

You may require advance notice of the need for victims of crime leave, where it is reasonable to do so. You can require the employee to give you, for each scheduled proceeding, a copy of the notice provided to the victim by the agency responsible for providing notice.

If the employee is unable to give advance notice, you may not take any action against the employee if he/she can provide certification of the need for leave within a reasonable amount of time after the absence.

Certification that is sufficient includes documentation of the judicial proceeding from:

- The court or government agency setting the hearing;
- The district attorney or prosecuting attorney's office; or
- The victim/witness office that is advocating on behalf of the victim.

You must maintain the confidentiality of requests for or documentation of violent crime leave.

Paying the Non-Exempt Employee

Non-exempt employees do not get paid for any time that they do not work. There is no legal requirement that you pay non-exempt employees who need time off for victims of crime leave.

You must allow, and may require, employees to use any accrued vacation, PTO, or other paid time off available to the them.

Paying the Exempt Employee

Exempt employees are subject to both state and federal law and you may not deduct from the salary of an exempt employee unless the employee has performed no work during the workday. The amount of time the employee works does not matter. The performance of any work during a workday in which the employee takes victims of crime leave requires payment of the employee's daily salary.

Continuing Benefits

You cannot discriminate against an eligible employee who takes victims of crime leave. Benefits should be handled the same as for employees who are absent for similar periods of time. If the employee is on paid leave, benefits typically continue at the same level as if the employee were at work.

Return to Work

You cannot discriminate against an eligible employee who takes victims of crime leave. Absent extenuating circumstances, such as layoffs or the employee's physical or mental inability to return to work, the employee must be reinstated to his/her job.

If you need to lay off an employee who is taking victims of crime leave, remember that the employee has the same rights and seniority as if he/she had been at work.

> If you need to terminate or lay off an employee who is taking victims of crime leave, consult legal counsel.

What You Should Do

1. Include in your employee handbook or written policy:
   - Any requirements for documentation of the judicial proceeding; and
   - Any requirements for using paid time off before taking unpaid time off.

> You cannot discriminate against someone for taking victims of crime leave. Any requirements to use paid time off should apply to all types of leave.

   For appropriate language, see the sample *Victims of Crime Leave Policy*, described in Table 23 on page 152.

2. Require documentation of the need for leave.

3. Pay the employee for vacation, PTO, or other paid time off, if you require it or the employee requests it.

4. Continue the employee's health benefits (if any) and notify the employee of any required payments.

5. Pay the exempt employee for any day in which he/she performs any work.

6. Reinstate the employee as required by law.

7. Make sure that the employee returning from leave receives all benefits and rights as if he/she had been continuously employed.

Reasonable Accommodation for Rehabilitation

Employees who voluntarily enter alcohol or drug rehabilitation are covered by the labor code as well as disability leave as a reasonable accommodation.

The Law Explained

Employers with five or more employees are required to reasonably accommodate an employee who wishes to voluntarily enter and participate in a drug or alcohol rehabilitation program. You must allow the employee such time off, which is typically unpaid, unless the leave would impose an undue hardship.[16]

Employees may file a complaint with the Labor Commissioner if they believe that they have been denied reasonable accommodation. You must make reasonable efforts to provide accommodation and safeguard the privacy of the employee, with regard to the fact that he/she has entered alcohol or drug rehabilitation.[17]

An employee who is absent for alcohol/drug rehab may use sick pay to which he/she is entitled.

Documentation

There is no provision in the law for requiring documentation. However, you can by policy require documentation of the employee's participation in a rehabilitation program, if you require certification for other types of disability leave.

---

16. Cal. Lab. Code sec. 1025
17. Cal. Lab. Code sec. 1026

 California Chamber of Commerce^{SM} 2005

Paying Non-Exempt Employees

There is no legal requirement that you pay non-exempt employees who are absent for this type of leave, unless they have sick pay or PTO available.[18] The employee may choose to use paid sick leave or PTO for the time he/she is absent and participating in rehabilitation.

Paying Exempt Employees

As a general rule, you must pay exempt employees for any day in which they perform any work. Thus you could not deduct from the exempt employee's salary for a partial day of absence to participate in rehab.

If the exempt employee is absent for a complete day or entire week, you may deduct from his/her salary for the absence. However, the employee may choose to use paid sick leave for the time he/she is absent and participating in rehab.

Continuing Benefits

You cannot discriminate against an employee who takes time off for alcohol and drug rehab. Benefits should be handled the same as for employees who are absent for similar periods of time. If the employee is also eligible for FMLA/CFRA leave, benefits would continue as if the employee were still on the payroll. If the employee is on paid leave, benefits typically continue at the same level as if the employee were at work.

Return to Work

You cannot discriminate against an employee who takes time off for the reasons stated above. Absent extenuating circumstances, such as layoffs or the employee's physical or mental inability to return to work, the employee must be reinstated to his/her job.

Consult with legal counsel before you terminate the employee based on your inability to provide reasonable accommodation because of undue hardship.

What You Should Do

1. Include in your employee handbook any certification requirements for any type of disability leave.

---

18. Cal. Lab. Code sec. 1027

2. Advise the employee seeking such leave of any such requirements.

3. Provide written notice if the leave will also be FMLA/CFRA running concurrently.

4. Include in your employee handbook any requirements to take paid leave.

5. Pay the employee sick leave if he/she has accrued sick leave.

Volunteer Civil Service Personnel Leave

Volunteer civil service personnel need to take time off to perform their emergency duties, and are protected by state law when they do so.[19] Volunteer civil service personnel are defined as volunteer firefighters, reserve peace officers, and emergency rescue personnel.

The Law Explained

All employers are prohibited from discharging or discriminating against an employee who takes time off to perform emergency duty as a volunteer firefighter, reserve peace officer, or emergency rescue personnel.

Employers with 50 or more employees must allow employees who are volunteer firefighters to take a temporary leave of absence to engage in fire or law enforcement training. The maximum amount of leave per calendar year is 14 days.[20]

Documentation

There is no provision in the law for required documentation. However, you can by policy require a written statement from the employee or, if possible, someone within the volunteer organization, to verify the need for leave.

Paying Non-Exempt Employees

There is no legal requirement that you pay non-exempt employees who serve as volunteers. Non-exempt employees may use (or you may require the use of) vacation, PTO or other paid time off that is available to the employee.

---

19. Cal. Lab. Code secs. 230.3
20. Cal. Lab. Code sec. 230.4

Paying Exempt Employees

As a general rule, you must pay exempt employees for any day in which they perform any work. Thus, you could not deduct from the exempt employee's salary for a partial day of absence for volunteer fire fighting, peace officer or emergency rescue personnel duties.

If the exempt employee is absent for an entire week or for complete days, you may deduct from his/her salary for an entire day or week of absence.

Continuing Benefits

You cannot discriminate against an employee who takes time off to serve as a volunteer for one of the reasons stated above. Benefits should be handled the same as for employees who are absent for similar periods of time. If the employee is on paid leave, benefits typically continue at the same level as if the employee were at work.

Return to Work

You cannot discriminate against an employee who takes time off for the reasons stated above. Absent extenuating circumstances, such as layoffs or the employee's physical or mental inability to return to work, the employee must be reinstated to his/her job.

What You Should Do

1. Let volunteer civil service personnel know to whom they should report the need to leave for duty.

2. Advise employees of any documentation requirements.

3. If you employ more than 50 employees, track the time spent in training by employees who are volunteer firefighters.

4. Include in your employee handbook any requirements to take paid leave. For appropriate language, see the sample *Volunteer Civil Service Personnel Policy*, described in Table 23 on page 153.

5. Pay exempt employees for any day in which they perform any work.

You cannot discriminate against someone for taking time off to respond to an emergency, or for training (employers with 50 or more employees). Any requirements to take paid leave should apply to all types of leave.

School Appearance Leave

Employees at certain times may need to appear at their child/ward's school in connection with disciplinary action by the school.

The Law Explained

The Education Code requires that parents or guardians attend class with the student when the student is suspended.

All employers are prohibited from discriminating against an employee who takes time off to appear at the school of their child or ward in connection with a suspension from a class or school.[21]

Documentation

The parent or guardian should receive a written notice from the school stating that they must attend a class. You may require a copy of the notice or some other certification from the school stating that the presence of your employee is required.

Paying Non-Exempt Employees

There is no legal requirement that you pay non-exempt employees who take time off to attend a class or school with a suspended child. Non-exempt employees may use (or you may require the use of) vacation, PTO, or other paid time off that is available to the employee.

Paying Exempt Employees

As a general rule, you must pay exempt employees for any day in which they perform any work. Thus you could not deduct from the exempt employee's salary for a partial day of absence to attend a child or ward's class or school. However, if the employee is absent for a complete day for personal reasons, you may deduct from his/her salary for a complete day of absence.

---

21. Cal. Lab. Code sec. 230.7

Continuing Benefits

You cannot discriminate against an employee who takes time off to attend a child or ward's class or school. Benefits should be handled the same as for employees who are absent for similar periods of time. If the employee is on paid leave, benefits typically continue at the same level as if the employee were at work.

Return to Work

You cannot discriminate against an employee who takes time off as required by a child's school. However, the employee has no greater right to his/her job than when the employee took time off.

What You Should Do

1. Put employees on notice of any documentation requirements.

2. Include in your employee handbook any requirements for the use of paid leave.

> You cannot discriminate against someone for taking time off to attend a child's class. Any requirements to take paid leave should apply to all types of leave.

3. Pay exempt employees for any day in which they perform any work.

School Activities Leave

Employees who are parents are allowed to participate in their children's activities at school.

The Law Explained

Employers with 25 or more employees must permit employees to take time off to participate in school activities with their child.[22]

Employees who are also the parent, guardian, or custodial grandparent of a child or children in kindergarten or grades 1 through 12, or a child in a licensed child day care

---

22. Cal. Lab. Code sec. 230.8

facility often wish to take time off to participate in school activities. However, the employee must follow these guidelines:

- The time does not exceed 40 hours per year, nor eight hours in a calendar month;
- The employee gives reasonable prior notice of the planned absence; and
- The employee provides documentation of the participation if required by the employer.

If both parents are employed by the same employer at the same worksite, you can limit the absence to the parent who first gave notice of the planned absence. A planned absence for a school activity by the other employee (parent) at the same time does not have to be given and you may require that the other employee receive your approval for the time off.

Documentation

If you require documentation of the employee's participation in a school activity, the employee must provide such proof. Acceptable documentation is whatever written verification of participation that the school or day care facility deems appropriate and reasonable.

Paying Non-Exempt Employees

There is no legal requirement that you pay non-exempt employees who take time off to participate in a school activity. Non-exempt employees may use (or you may require the use of) vacation, PTO, or other paid time off that is available to the employee.

Paying Exempt Employees

As a general rule, you must pay exempt employees for any day in which they perform any work. Thus you could not deduct from the exempt employee's salary for a partial day of absence to participate in a school activity. However, if the employee is absent for a complete day to participate in a school activity, you may deduct from their salary for the complete day of absence.

Continuing Benefits

You cannot discriminate against an employee who takes time off for school activities, as long as the time does not exceed that allowed by the law. Benefits should be handled the same as for employees who are absent for similar periods of time. If the employee is on paid leave, benefits typically continue at the same level as if the employee were at work.

Return to Work

You cannot discriminate against an employee who takes time off to attend his/her child's school activities. Absent extenuating circumstances, such as layoffs, or the employee's physical or mental inability to return to work, the employee must be reinstated to his/her job.

What You Should Do

If you employ more than 25 employees, you should:

1. Advise employees of any documentation requirements for school activity leave.

2. Include in your employee handbook any requirements for the use of paid leave before taking unpaid leave. For appropriate language, see the sample *School Activities Policy*, described in Table 23 on page 152.

> You cannot discriminate against someone for taking school activity leave. The required use of paid time off should apply to all absences.

3. Pay exempt employees for any day in which they perform any work.

4. Track the amount of time taken by employees, and advise employees when they reach the limit of eight hours in a calendar month or 40 hours in a year.

Voting Leave

If an employee does not have sufficient time outside of working hours to vote in a statewide election, you must provide paid time off for the employee to vote.

The Law Explained

Employees have an absolute right to vote, and the Election Code provides for up to two hours of paid leave when the employee's work schedule does not allow him/her enough time to vote.[23]

The two hours provided may be at the beginning or end of the employee's regular working shift, whichever allows the employee the most free time to vote, and the least time off from working.

Documentation

The employee must notify you at least two working days in advance to arrange a voting time. You must post information about voting rights in a conspicuous place at least 10 days before every statewide election.

What You Should Do

1. Post the *Time Off for Voting* notice 10 days prior to any statewide election. This notice is part of the **_Employer Poster_**, available from the California Chamber of Commerce.

2. Most employees have ample time outside of work to vote in statewide elections. However, if you have employees who work a 10- or 12-hour shift, or employees whose commute is such that they would not have time to vote outside of working hours, they may need time off.

3. You determine whether the time is to be taken at the beginning or the end of the shift. Be sure to advise the employee of which one you choose.

4. For language you can use in your employee handbook, see the sample *Time Off for Voting Policy*, described in Table 23 on page 152.

An exempt employee is paid for any day in which he/she performs any work. However, be sure that any non-exempt employees who need time off to vote are paid for the time missed from work, up to a maximum of two hours.

Employee Literacy Assistance

Employers with 25 or more employees must reasonably accommodate and assist an employee who reveals a problem of illiteracy and requests assistance.

---

23. Cal. Elec. Code sec. 14350

The Law Explained

There is no legal requirement that you provide a leave of absence for someone who requires assistance in enrolling in an adult literacy education program.

If you are willing to help, assistance might include providing the employee with the locations of local literacy education programs, or arranging for a literacy education provider to visit the workplace. If an employee needs time off from work in order to attend classes or seek other assistance (and such accommodation does not impose an undue hardship on you), you should provide the time off from work.

Employee Protection

You must make all reasonable efforts to safeguard the privacy of the employee who discloses a problem with illiteracy.

The employee who discloses a problem of illiteracy and who satisfactorily performs his/her job cannot be subject to termination because of the disclosure of illiteracy

Paying Non-Exempt Employees

The time off would be unpaid for non-exempt employees, although they could use any vacation or other paid time off that is available to them.

Paying Exempt Employees

An exempt employee must be paid for any day in which he/she performs any work, but deductions could be made from their salary for a complete day of absence. The exempt employee could use any vacation or other paid time off that is available when absent for a complete day.

Return to Work

Time off to seek such assistance should not impact the employee's benefits or right to return to work.

What You Should Do

If you employ 25 or more employees and an employee seeks assistance because of illiteracy, you should provide as much assistance as possible. This might include making phone calls to find a program or bringing someone into the workplace who can provide such assistance.

You are not obligated to pay employees for the time they spend attending classes. If the employee needs time off from work and it does not impose a hardship on you, you should provide time off. Non-exempt employees need not be paid for time not worked.

You may require the use of paid time off before an employee takes unpaid time off. If you require the use of paid time off, you should put the employee on notice of such a requirement and have a policy that requires the use of paid time off for all types of absences.

Forms and Checklists

New for 2005 The following table describes forms associated with protected leaves of absence.

You can find these forms on the CD included with this product.

Table 23. Forms and Checklists

Form name	What do I use it for?	When do I use it?	Who fills it out?	Where does it go?
Domestic Violence/Sexual Assault Victims Leave Policy (1-24 Employees) **New for 2005**	To inform employees about their rights to this type of leave and how your company handles it.	At time of hire and whenever you update the policy.	No filling out needed; you develop your policy based on this sample.	In your employee handbook; if you don't have a handbook, give a copy to every employee.

Table 23. Forms and Checklists *(continued)*

Form name	What do I use it for?	When do I use it?	Who fills it out?	Where does it go?
Domestic Violence/Sexual Assault Victims Leave Policy (25 or More Employees) **New for 2005**	To inform employees about their rights to this type of leave and how your company handles it.	At time of hire and whenever you update the policy.	No filling out needed; you develop your policy based on this sample.	In your employee handbook; if you don't have a handbook, give a copy to every employee.
Jury Duty and Witness Leave Policy	To inform employees about their rights to this type of leave and how your company handles it.	At time of hire and whenever you update the policy.	No filling out needed; you develop your policy based on this sample.	In your employee handbook; if you don't have a handbook, give a copy to every employee.
Military Leave Policy	To inform employees about their rights to this type of leave and how your company handles it.	At time of hire and whenever you update the policy.	No filling out needed; you develop your policy based on this sample.	In your employee handbook; if you don't have a handbook, give a copy to every employee.
School Activities Policy	To inform employees about their rights to this type of leave and how your company handles it.	At time of hire and whenever you update the policy.	No filling out needed; you develop your policy based on this sample.	In your employee handbook; if you don't have a handbook, give a copy to every employee.
Time Off for Voting Policy	To inform employees about their rights to this type of leave and how your company handles it.	At time of hire and whenever you update the policy.	No filling out needed; you develop your policy based on this sample.	In your employee handbook; if you don't have a handbook, give a copy to every employee.
Victims of Crime Leave Policy	To inform employees about their rights to this type of leave and how your company handles it.	At time of hire and whenever you update the policy.	No filling out needed; you develop your policy based on this sample.	In your employee handbook; if you don't have a handbook, give a copy to every employee.

Table 23. Forms and Checklists *(continued)*

Form name	What do I use it for?	When do I use it?	Who fills it out?	Where does it go?
Volunteer Civil Service Personnel Policy	To inform employees about their rights to this type of leave and how your company handles it.	At time of hire and whenever you update the policy.	No filling out needed; you develop your policy based on this sample.	In your employee handbook; if you don't have a handbook, give a copy to every employee.

Chapter 10
Other Optional Leaves

There are no laws that require you to offer time off, either paid or unpaid, other than those discussed in previous chapters. However, employers often wish to provide additional benefits in order to attract and retain their workforce. This chapter includes examples of other types of benefits that you may offer, and information on how to manage them, including any wage and hour issues. Vacation and paid time off (PTO) are discussed in Chapter 8, "Vacation and Paid Time Off."

 The forms mentioned in this chapter are on the CD included with this product.

Holidays and Personal Holidays

You may choose to give some or none of the more commonly celebrated holidays, such as New Year's Day, President's Day, Memorial Day, Independence Day, Labor Day, Veteran's Day, Thanksgiving, the Friday after Thanksgiving, Christmas Eve, and Christmas Day.

If you do offer paid holidays, you choose the ones that you observe. Eligibility requirements, and any requirements for the payment (such as employees must work the day before or after a holiday, or be on an approved, paid leave in order to be eligible for holiday pay) are also determined by you.

Depending on your business, you may not be able to give everyone a holiday at a specific time during the year.

> **Example:** Retail stores typically do not allow anyone to take off the Friday after Thanksgiving.

If commonly celebrated holidays occur during your busiest season, or if you merely want to give more flexibility to employees who celebrate other holidays, you may decide to designate a specific number of personal holidays.

The Law Explained

There are no legal requirements for employers in the private sector to provide holidays–either paid or unpaid. In the public sector (city, county, state and federal government) legally mandated holidays have been set by law.

Wage and Hour Issues – Holidays

The holidays that you observe are set by you. Since a paid holiday falls on a specific date, an individual who is not employed on that date does not earn or accrue pay for that holiday. There is no requirement that you pay out holidays at termination.

> **Example:** If you offer Thanksgiving and the Friday after as paid holidays, the employee who terminates on November 15th is not eligible for holiday pay for those two days. He/she was not employed at the time the paid holidays occurred.

You may set eligibility requirements for non-exempt employees to receive holiday pay, such as they must work the day before and/or the day after a holiday in order to receive pay. An exception might be if they were on approved paid leave (vacation/PTO/sick leave).

Or, you might require that a non-exempt employee work for you for some specified period of time before being eligible for holiday pay.

> **Example:** You can set up a policy that non-exempt employees are not eligible for holiday pay during their first 30 days of employment.

Exempt employees must be paid if they are ready, willing, and able to work and no work is available, such as a holiday when the company is shut down. You would not be able to withhold holiday pay from an exempt employee as you would for the non-exempt employee.

> **Example:** An exempt employee has been with you for less than 30 days. Your office is closed for two days for Thanksgiving and the Friday after. You would have to pay the exempt employee holiday pay, because he/she was ready, willing, and able to work those two days that you were closed.

Wage and Hour Issues – Personal Holidays

Personal holidays are treated differently and wage and hour laws do govern payment for the time at termination.

If the holiday is tied to a specific event, such as the employee's birthday or anniversary with the company, you may restrict the use of the holiday to a specific time period.

Example: You provide a personal holiday for an employee's anniversary of employment with the company, and the anniversary date is June 1. You may require that the employee take the holiday during a specified time period, such as the week before, the week of, or the week after the anniversary date. Failure to take the holiday during that time period can result in forfeiture. The forfeiture is possible because the holiday is tied to the occurrence of a specific event-the employee's anniversary date.

If the employee is not employed by you at the time he/she could have taken the personal holiday, you are not required to pay the holiday out at termination. However, if the employee terminates within the time period you allow for the use of the holiday, he/she should be paid at termination for the unused personal holiday.

What You Should Do

1. If you offer paid holidays as a benefit, you should include in your written policy/employee handbook:

    - The specific days that are observed as paid holidays;

    - Any requirements for payment for non-exempt employees, such as they must work the day before and/or the day after the holiday or be on an approved leave (sick/PTO/vacation);

    - A statement that employees who are not employed at the time the holiday is observed are not paid holiday pay; and

    - A statement that unused holidays do not accrue and are not paid out at termination.

2. If the nature of your business requires employees to work holidays, you determine the options available to employees. For example:

    - Pay for all hours worked and eight hours of holiday pay at straight time;

    - Pay for all hours worked and another day off in lieu of the holiday pay; and

    - Pay for all hours worked at a premium rate of pay (not because it is overtime but because the employee is working on a paid holiday), and eight hours of holiday pay at straight time or another day off in lieu of the holiday pay.

3. If you decide to provide personal holidays as a benefit for your employees, you should:

- Define the number of days employees receive;

- Include in your written policy/employee handbook, any designation of the time, such as "a paid day off for you birthday, your anniversary with the company," etc.; and

- Include in your policy any restrictions on the use of the holiday, such as, the day must be used the week before, the week of or the week after your anniversary date with the company. Failure to use the day off during that time results in loss of the holiday.

4. For language suitable for your employee handbook, see the sample *Holiday Policy*, described in Table 24 on page 167.

Floating Holidays

A floating holiday is one that is given to the employee to use at his/her discretion and is not tied to a specific event.

The Law Explained

Floating holidays can be used for any reason and they are treated the same as vacation and PTO. Like vacation and PTO, you may place a reasonable cap on the accrual of floating holidays.

Example: You decide to give employees three floating holidays per year. They accrue at the rate of two hours per month, so that an employee earns one floating holiday after four months of employment, a second one after eight months, and the third after 12 months. Your policy states that employees may carry over two days, or 16 hours, of floating holidays each year. You may cap the accrual of floating holidays so that the employee who does not use his/her floating holidays in one year, will not earn any more time the following year until he/she has taken one or more days of floating holidays.

Alternatively, you may require that employees use all floating holidays in the year in which they are earned. This requires you to closely monitor the use of the holidays and "remind" employees that they need to take the time off before the end of the time period you use for accrual.

Other options would be to pay the employee at the end of the year for any accrued and unused floating holidays, or to allow the employee to carry over all accrued and unused time.

If you offer floating holidays, the best way to control costs is to choose an option other than allowing unlimited accrual. As with vacation and PTO, a floating holiday is earned at the employee's current rate of pay. However, the payout for these types of benefits is typically at a higher rate, because it must be paid at the employee's rate of pay at termination.

The decision is yours to make as to offering or not offering floating holidays. If you decide to offer them, you determine:

- Who is eligible;
- The accrual rate;
- Any restrictions as to time, such as no holidays or vacation may be taken during your busy season; and
- Any requirements that the holiday must be used or:
    - It is paid out; or
    - There is a cap on the accrual if the employee does not take some amount of the accrued time. You decide on what the cap amount will be.

Religious Accommodation and Floating Holidays

If you have a particularly diverse workforce in terms of race, religion, or national origin, you might have noticed that not all employees celebrate the same "national holidays."

What do you do if you have a workforce with a large number of employees who celebrate a specific holiday, and they all want to take a day off on the same date? You may consider closing down for the day, but for most employers that is not an option.

If the holiday is a religious one, you are required by law to provide reasonable accommodation for religious reasons. Closing your business is usually not reasonable. However, you may limit the number of employees who can be gone from the company, from a department, a specific job, etc. Employees could take a floating holiday based on seniority, by a random drawing or some other means of choosing a limited number of employees.

Wage and Hour Issues

Since the floating holiday may be taken at any time and has no restrictions on its use, it is treated the same as vacation and PTO. The time must accrue, it must vest and it must be paid out at termination if unused.

Employees may file a wage and hour claim with the state Labor Commissioner or in Superior Court if you fail to pay out accrued and unused floating holiday wages at termination. If the employee wins, he/she may collect a waiting penalty of one day's wage for every day (up to 30) that the wages were unpaid. The employee can go back in time for up to 4 years for unpaid wages.

However, if you have an illegal "use it or lose it" policy, there is no statute of limitations on such a claim.

What You Should Do

1. Determine the number of floating holidays to be earned, if any, and include this information in your employee handbook or other written policy, along with:

    - Any caps on accrual, or required use or payout during the year;
    - Any eligibility requirements; and
    - Any restrictions on the use of the time, such as no one can take time off during your busy season.

2. Track employee use of floating holidays. Pay out any accrued and unused time at termination.

Bereavement Leave

Bereavement leave is time off for an employee whose family member has died. Companies that provide bereavement leave offer anywhere from one day to five days of paid leave. Some offer additional leave that is unpaid, depending on the circumstances, such as distance that must be traveled, or employees who have been designated as the executor of the estate and must perform those duties. You determine not only whether time off is granted, but also how much, and whether it is paid, unpaid, or a combination of both.

The Law Explained

There is no legal requirement that you provide such time, but if you choose to do so, the amount of time, the family members covered, and the payment for time is determined by your policy.

Wage and Hour Issues

Non-exempt employees do not have to be paid for any time that they do not work, including partial days of absence.

Exempt employees must be paid for any day in which they perform any work. If an exempt employee takes off half a day to attend a funeral, the employee must be paid for the entire day, whether you offer paid time off or not. If the exempt employee is absent for a full day or more, you may deduct from his/her salary in increments of a full day or more.

> ***Example:*** An exempt employee requests leave to attend the funeral of his mother, who lived in another state. You grant the leave, but remind the employee that your policy provides for up to five days of paid bereavement leave. The employee asks for an additional two workdays, because of the travel involved. You grant two days of unpaid bereavement leave. If the exempt employee does not work on those two days, you do not have to pay him/her for that time. Under your policy, you pay for five working days of bereavement leave and the employee takes two unpaid days. As an alternative, the exempt employee might request to use paid time off, such as vacation or PTO.

Documentation

You may, by policy, require documentation of the fact that the deceased was related to (a "family member" of) your employee. Examples include a death notice from a newspaper or a memorial card from the funeral home.

What You Should Do

If you offer bereavement leave, include the following in your written policy or employee handbook:

- Whether the time off is paid or unpaid;
- How much time is provided;

- Any restrictions on the amount of time that can be taken (for example, in a calendar year);
- The definition of "family" for the purpose of bereavement leave; and
- Specific requirements for requesting such a leave or for designating an absence as bereavement leave, such as specific forms to request the time off, or documentation requirements.

Some suggestions for the definition of "family" include an employee's:

- Spouse, domestic partner, or someone who stands in substantially the same relationship;
- Son or daughter;
- Ex-spouse or partner who is the father/mother of the employee's child;
- Father or mother;
- Stepparent;
- Brother or sister;
- Father or mother-in-law;
- Grandchild;
- Grandparent; or
- Anyone with whom the employee had an "in loco parentis" relationship — that is, the employee was a "parent" to the deceased or the deceased was a "parent" to the employee.

For language suitable for your employee handbook, see the sample *Bereavement Leave Policy*, described in Table 24 on page 167.

Unpaid Personal Leave

Employers who are not subject to family medical leave or who merely wish to provide time off for other reasons may choose to grant unpaid personal leave. Reasons for such leave might include:

- Illness or injury of the employee that exceeds any time under your policy or that is required by law;
- The need to care for a family member that exceeds any time under your policy or that is required by law, or for a family member not covered by policy or by law;

- Staying home with a newborn child beyond the period allowed by PDL or FMLA/CFRA;

- Time needed by an employee who is not eligible for family medical leave;

- Time for an employee to travel home to visit where the distance is such that normal vacation time is not sufficient; or

- The trip of a lifetime, for which the employee does not have enough vacation to cover all of the time needed.

You decide whether or not you wish to provide such time off, any eligibility requirements such as length of service, the amount of time that is available, what benefits will be continued, if any, and reinstatement rights, if any.

The Law Explained

There is no law that requires you to provide unpaid personal leave. You decide whether or not to offer such a benefit. If you do offer unpaid personal time as a benefit, you should document any requirements or restrictions (see suggestions below) and apply them fairly and evenly to all employees covered by the benefit.

Since this is unpaid time, do not pay the employee. The exception would be where an exempt employee performs some work, he/she must be paid for the full day if they perform any work in that day.

What You Should Do

If you offer unpaid personal leave, include in your employee handbook or other written policy:

- Eligibility requirements, such as length of service;

- The maximum amount of time that you grant as unpaid personal leave;

- The reasons for which you grant the leave;

- Any restrictions on the use of such leave, such as no more than three times in five years;

- Any conditions or approval requirements (for example, the leave requires the approval of the employee's supervisor and the Plant Superintendent);

- What benefits will continue (if any), payments required by the employee, and how and when the payments are to be made;

- Any impact on seniority or pension benefits;
- Any impact on benefit accrual (such as vacation and sick leave); and
- Any reinstatement rights, or lack of reinstatement rights.

Unpaid Sick Leave

You may choose to offer an extension to paid sick leave or only unpaid sick leave. There are times when an employee may exhaust all sick leave and you wish to give them additional time off to recover.

The Law Explained

There is no law that requires you to provide unpaid sick leave. You decide whether or not to offer such a benefit. If you do offer unpaid sick leave as a benefit, you should document any requirements or restrictions (see suggestions below) and apply them fairly and evenly to all employees covered by the benefit.

Since this is unpaid time, you do not pay the employee. The exception would be where an exempt employee performs some work. He/she must be paid for the full day if he/she performs any work in that day.

What You Should Do

If you offer unpaid sick leave, include in your employee handbook or other written policy:

- Eligibility requirements, such as length of service;
- The amount of time that is available;
- What benefits are continued, if any, and any required payments;
- The impact on seniority and benefit accrual such as vacation and paid sick leave;
- Any issues related to pension benefits; and
- Reinstatement rights, if any.

Sabbaticals

A sabbatical leave is usually associated with academia and professors who have long tenure with a college or university. In the past, strong unions bargained for sabbaticals as a reward for length of service in an organization.

The decision to offer a sabbatical is yours to make. A sabbatical can be paid or unpaid, but it is an extension of vacation that is usually associated with some length of service. Some sabbaticals are given so that the employee can just take time off, or to continue his/her education or advanced training.

The Law Explained

There is no law that requires you to provide sabbatical leave. You decide whether or not to offer such a benefit. If you do offer sabbatical leave as a benefit, you should document any requirements or restrictions (see suggestions below) and apply them fairly and evenly to all employees covered by the benefit.

Non-exempt employees need not be paid if they are not working.

Exempt employees must be paid at least the minimum salary requirement ($2,340 a month) if you wish to maintain their exempt status and you are expecting that they perform some work. If the sabbatical involves no work or training on the part of the employee, no compensation would be required, it would simply be unpaid leave.

What You Should Do

If you offer sabbaticals, include in your employee handbook or other written policy:

- Any length of service requirements;
- Whether the sabbatical is paid or unpaid time;
- Any qualifiers, such as sabbaticals only offered to employees who have achieved a performance rating of "Outstanding" or better, or only offered to employees who are managers and above, or available only if the leave is to continue the employee's training;
- The length of time the employee may take leave from work;
- Continuation of vacation and/or sick leave accrual and health benefits; and
- Seniority, pension, and reinstatement rights.

Education Leave

If continuing education or higher education is a desirable goal for your employees, and you want to encourage employees, you may wish to offer some period of time off from work for this purpose.

The Law Explained

There is no law that requires you to provide education leave. You decide whether or not to offer such a benefit. If you do offer education leave as a benefit, you should document any requirements or restrictions (see suggestions below) and apply them fairly and evenly to all employees covered by the benefit.

If you are requiring that employees take specific training or courses or complete a degree program that is related to their job or that will benefit you, you are required to pay them for their time spent in training, as well as the training itself.

If the employee is being given time off to take courses or complete a degree program that is not related to what they currently do or will not lead to a promotion, there is no requirement that you pay them or that you pay for their tuition and books.

What You Should Do

If you offer education leave, include in your employee handbook or other written policy:

- Employee eligibility requirements;
- The amount of time allowed, and any restrictions, such as no more than one year of leave;
- Whether the time is paid or unpaid;
- What types of training or courses might be covered;
- Any requirements for completion of a specific degree or course program;
- Any limits on the number of times an employee can take such a leave;
- Continuation of vacation and/or sick leave accrual and health benefits; and
- Seniority, pension, and reinstatement rights.

For language suitable for your employee handbook, see the sample *External Employee Education Policy*, described in Table 24.

Forms and Checklists

New for 2005 The following table describes forms associated with optional leaves of absence.

 You can find these forms on the CD included with this product.

Table 24. Forms and Checklists

Form name	What do I use it for?	When do I use it?	Who fills it out?	Where does it go?
Bereavement Leave Policy	To inform employees about the bereavement leave you offer and requirements for its use.	At time of hire and whenever you update the policy.	No filling out needed; you develop your policy based on this sample.	In your employee handbook; if you don't have a handbook, give a copy to every employee.
External Employee Education Policy	To inform employees about the education leave you offer and requirements for its use.	At time of hire and whenever you update the policy.	No filling out needed; you develop your policy based on this sample.	In your employee handbook; if you don't have a handbook, give a copy to every employee.
Holiday Policy	To inform employees about the holidays you offer and requirements for its use.	At time of hire and whenever you update the policy.	No filling out needed; you develop your policy based on this sample.	In your employee handbook; if you don't have a handbook, give a copy to every employee.

Index

A

Acknowledgement of Receipt of Notification of COBRA Rights, information on, 12

ADA. *See* Americans with Disabilities Act

Adult literacy education program, 150

Alcohol rehabilitation, leave for, 141–143

Alternative work schedule, and calculating family medical leave, 46

Americans with Disabilities Act (ADA) (1990), 71, 75

B

Baby bonding family leave
　See also Family medical leave
　duration of, 45–55
　interaction with pregnancy disability leave, 25–26
　medical certification for, 50
　paid family leave benefits during, 29
　using vacation during, 29

Bargaining, collective. *See* Collective bargaining

Base period, for state disability insurance benefits, 118

Benefits
　during disability leave, 80
　during domestic violence victim leave, 136
　during family medical leave, 62–64
　during jury duty leave, 133
　during military service leave, 129–130
　during paid time off, 125
　during personal leave of absence, 163–164
　during pregnancy disability leave, 30–32
　during school activities leave, 147
　during school appearance leave, 146
　during sexual assault victim leave, 136
　during sick leave, 118–119
　during vacation, 125
　during volunteer civil service leave, 144
　during witness duty leave, 133
　pamphlet describing, 87

Bereavement leave
　definition of, 160
　documentation for, 161
　duration of, 160
　eligibility for, 160–162
　employee handbook on, 161–162
　forms related to, 167
　legal requirements for, 161
　pay during, 161

Bereavement Leave Policy, information on, 162, 167

Breast milk, expressing at work, 34

C

Cal-COBRA - Notice to Carrier, information on, 12

Cal-COBRA - Notice to Employee, information on, 13

Cal-COBRA. *See* Consolidated Omnibus Budget Reconciliation Act

California Family Rights Act (CFRA) (1991)
See also Family and Medical Leave Act; Family medical leave; Pregnancy disability leave
counting employees toward threshold for, 43
defined, 43
interaction with FMLA, 4
on employee notice of need for leave, 48–50
on employee right to family medical leave, 43

California Family Rights Act and Pregnancy Disability Poster, information on, 18, 19, 22, 35, 36, 47, 48, 52

Certification of Health Care Provider – WH 380, information on, 50

Certification of Physician or Practitioner for Employee Return to Work, information on, 32, 36, 67, 81

Certification of Physician or Practitioner for PDL or PDL/FMLA, information on, 21, 22, 36

Certification of Physician or Practitioner for Transfer Due to Pregnancy Disability, information on, 21, 22, 36

CFRA. *See* California Family Rights Act

Children of employees
and domestic violence victim leave, 135
and school activities leave, 146–148
and school appearance leave, 145–146
family medical leave to care for, 44
kin care to care for, 115
medical certification for, 50, 51, 117
serious health condition of, 44

Claims, wage and hour, 125, 160

COBRA Continuation Coverage Election Notice (California Employees), information on, 13

COBRA Continuation Coverage Election Notice (Outside California), information on, 14

COBRA – Notice to Plan Administrator, information on, 14

COBRA. *See* Consolidated Omnibus Budget Reconciliation Act

Collective bargaining
and comparable positions, 33
and seniority, 30, 63
and transfers, 21

Comparable position
availability of, 33
definition of, 33, 65
for employee returning from military service leave, 130
guaranteed reinstatement to, 64

Compensation. *See* Wage(s)

Confidentiality
of medical certifications, 27, 53
of reason for family medical leave, 49

Consolidated Omnibus Budget Reconciliation Act (COBRA) (1985), 12–14, 31, 64, 80, 94, 95, 119, 129

Coordination of PDL with Family/Medical Leave Policy (50 or More Employees), information on, 19, 37, 76

Crime victims, notice for, and workers' compensation, 87, 88

D

Death
of employee, 90
of employee family member. *See* Bereavement leave

Disabilities
definition of, 72–73
exclusions from, 73
military-related, 130–131
reasonable accommodation for. *See* Reasonable accommodation

Disability leave
administration of, 78–79
as reasonable accommodation, 71, 78–79
benefits during, 80
employers who must provide, 75
forms related to, 82
interaction with family medical leave, 4, 77, 78

interaction with pregnancy disability leave, 4
interaction with workers' compensation, 4, 80
medical certification for, 77
pay during, 79–80
poster requirements for, 75
purposes of, 75
qualifying events, 75
reinstatement after, 81
    guarantee of, 79
    refusal of, 81
request for, 76–77
state disability insurance benefits during, 79
summary of requirements for, 71–72
termination of employee on, 79
transfer during, 81
using paid leave during, 80

Discharge. *See* Termination

Discrimination and Harassment in Employment are Prohibited by Law, information on, 76

Doctor's First Report of Occupational Injury or Illness, information on, 91, 96

Doctors. *See* Health care providers

Domestic partners of employees
and bereavement leave, 162
and paid family leave benefits, 61
family medical leave to care for, 44, 56–57, 111
kin care to care for, 115
medical certification for, 51, 117
serious health condition of, 44

Domestic violence victim leave
administration of, 137–138
benefits during, 136
definition of, 134
documentation for, 135–136
eligibility for, 135
forms related to, 151, 152
pay during, 136
reinstatement after, 137

Domestic Violence/Sexual Assault Victims Leave Policy (1-24 Employees), information on, 137

Domestic Violence/Sexual Assault Victims Leave Policy (25 or More Employees), information on, 137

Domestic Violence/Sexual Assault Victims Leave Policy, information on, 151, 152

Drug abuse, excluded as a disability, 73

Drug rehabilitation, leave for, 141–143

E

EDD. *See* Employment Development Department

Education leave
See also Literacy assistance; Training; Training time
definition of, 166
employee handbook on, 166
for optional courses, 166
for required courses, 166
forms related to, 167

Emergency service personnel
definition of, 143
volunteer civil service leave for, 143–144

Employee handbooks
on bereavement leave, 161–162
on coordinating paid time off with state benefits, 123
on coordinating vacation with state benefits, 123
on education leave, 166
on floating holidays, 160
on paid holidays, 157
on paid time off, 122, 125
on personal holidays, 158
on personal leaves of absence, 163–164
on pregnancy disability leave, 19, 31
on sabbaticals, 165
on sick leave, 117, 119
on training, 166
on unpaid sick leave, 164
on vacation, 122, 125

Employee Letter - CFRA Leave Taken after FMLA/PDL, information on, 19, 23, 27, 37, 52, 60

Index

Employee Letter - FMLA/CFRA, information on, 52, 60, 68, 77

Employee Letter - PDL Only, information on, 19, 23, 26, 37, 52, 60

Employee Letter - PDL/FMLA, information on, 19, 23, 27, 37, 60

Employee Retirement Income Security Act (ERISA) (1974), 121

Employee's Claim for Workers' Compensation Benefits (DWC 1), information on, 90, 91, 96

Employer's Report of Occupational Injury or Illness (Form 5020), information on, 90, 91, 97

Employment Development Department (EDD), 62, 101, 102, 104, 106

Equal Employment Opportunity Commission (EEOC), 74

Equal Employment Opportunity is the Law, information on, 75, 76

Equal Employment Opportunity Policy (5 or More Employees), information on, 75, 82

ERISA. *See* Employee Retirement Income Security Act

Essential job functions
 definition of, 73
 determining, 74

Exclusive remedy, workers' compensation as, 84

External Employee Education Policy, information on, 166, 167

F

Fair Employment and Housing Act (FEHA) (1980), 75

Family and Medical Leave Act (FMLA) (1993)
 See also California Family Rights Act; Family medical leave; Pregnancy disability leave
 counting employees toward threshold for, 43
 interaction with CFRA, 3
 on employee notice of need for leave, 48–50
 on employee right to family medical leave, 43
 on refusal to reinstate "key" employee, 65–66

Family medical leave
 See also California Family Rights Act; Family and Medical Leave Act; Pregnancy disability leave
 administration of, 53–59
 and domestic partners, 44, 56–57, 111
 and reduced work schedule, 46
 benefits during, 62–64
 calculation of, 45–47
 denying, 49
 designating leave as
  after employee's return to work, 58–59
  after leave commences, 58
  employer responsibility for, 59
  upon notice of need for, 57–59
 eligibility for, 43–44
 employee waiver of rights to, 49
 employers who must provide, 43
 for part-time employees, 46
 forms related to, 68–69
 holidays during, 59
 interaction with disability leave, 3, 4, 77, 78
 interaction with kin care, 118
 interaction with pregnancy disability leave, 3, 4, 26
 interaction with workers' compensation, 3, 4
 intermittent, 46, 55
 layoffs during, 67
 medical certification for, 50–51, 52–53, 57
 notice requirements for, 48
 paid family leave benefits during, 61–62
 pay during, 60–62
 poster requirements for, 47–48
 purposes of, 43
 qualifying events, 44
 reinstatement after, 64
  refusal of, 65–66, 66
  to comparable position, 65
  to different position, 65
 request for, 48–53
 serious health condition, definition of, 44–45

state disability insurance benefits during, 60-62
summary of requirements for, 41-42
termination of employee on, 51, 64, 66, 67
using paid leave during, 58, 61-62
using paid time off during, 122
using sick leave during, 118
using vacation during, 122

Family/Medical Leave Policy (50 or More Employees), information on, 19, 68, 76

Federal Employment and Housing Commission (FEHC), 74

Federal Family and Medical Leave Act Poster, information on, 18, 47, 52, 68, 69

Floating holidays
accrual of, 158, 159, 160
as religious accommodation, 159
definition of, 158
eligibility for, 159
employee handbook on, 160
failure to pay for accrued, 160
forfeiture of, 158
pay for unused, 159, 160
timing of, 159

FMLA. *See* Family and Medical Leave Act

FMLA/CFRA Checklist for Employer Compliance, information on, 42, 53, 69

For Your Benefit, California's Program for the Unemployed (Form 2320), information on, 22, 76, 113

G

Guidelines for Determining OSHA Log 300 Recordability, information on, 91, 97

H

Health care providers
definition of, 51
medical certification from. *See* Medical certification

Health insurance
during family medical leave, 63
during military service leave, 129
during pregnancy disability leave, 30

Holiday Policy, information on, 158, 167

Holidays
See also Floating holidays; Personal holidays
during family medical leave, 59
eligibility for, 155, 156
employee handbook on, 157
forms related to, 167
most commonly granted, 155
pay for unused, 156
pay options for, 157
paying exempt employees for, 156
paying non-exempt employees for, 156
religious, 159
unpaid, 156

I

Injury and Illness Incident Report (Form 301), information on, 91, 97

J

Jury Duty and Witness Leave Policy, information on, 134, 152

Jury duty leave
administration of, 134
benefits during, 133
definition of, 132
documentation for, 133
eligibility for, 132
forms related to, 152
pay during, 133
reinstatement after, 133-134

K

"Key" employees, 65-66

Kin care
  See also Sick leave
  administration of, 117
  amount of sick leave available as, 115, 116
  and paid time off, 123
  eligibility for, 116
  forms related to, 120
  interaction with family medical leave, 118
  medical certification for, 117
  paid family leave benefits during, 118
  purposes of, 115
  reinstatement after, 119
  request for, 116–117

L

Labor Commissioner, and wage and hour claims, 125, 160

Lactation accommodation, 34

Layoffs
  during family medical leave, 67
  during pregnancy disability leave, 34

Leaves of Absence Policy, information on, 31, 95, 97

Literacy assistance
  and privacy of employees, 150
  employers who must provide, 149
  leave for, 150
    legal requirements for, 150
    pay during, 150, 151
    reinstatement after, 150
  providing to employees, 151
  types of, 150

Log of Work-Related Injuries and Illnesses (Form 300), information on, 91, 97

M

Major life activities, definition of, 73

Medical certification
  for baby bonding family leave, 50
  for disability leave, 77
  for domestic violence victim leave, 136
  for family medical leave, 50–51, 52–53, 57
  for kin care, 117
  for pregnancy disability leave, 20–21
  for sexual assault victim leave, 136
  for sick leave, 116, 117
  of need for reasonable accommodation, 81
  privacy of, 27, 53

Medical Certification - FMLA/CFRA, information on, 50, 52, 69, 77, 105

Military Leave Policy, information on, 131, 152

Military service leave
  administration of, 131–132
  benefits during, 129–130
  definition of, 127
  documentation for, 128–129
  duration of, 128
  eligibility for, 127–128
  forms related to, 152
  pay during, 129
  poster requirements for, 127
  reinstatement after, 130–131
    and reasonable accommodation, 130–131
    to comparable position, 130

N

Notice of Employee Death (DIA 510), information on, 91, 98

Notice to Employee as to Change in Relationship, information on, 23, 38, 53, 78, 113

Notice to Employees: Unemployment Insurance, State Disability Insurance, and Paid Family Leave (DE 1857A), information on, 104, 109, 113

Notices
  for crime victims, and workers' compensation, 88
  for family medical leave, 48
  for paid family leave, 109
  for paid time off, 122
  for pregnancy disability leave, 18–19
  for sick leave, 116
  for state disability insurance, 104
  for vacation, 122

O

Optional Worksheet to Help You Fill Out the Annual Summary (Form 300A), information on, 91, 98

P

Paid Family Leave (DE 2511), information on, 22, 52, 109, 113

Paid family leave (PFL) benefits
    and paid time off, 123
    and vacation, 123
    during baby bonding family leave, 29
    during family medical leave, 61–62
    during kin care, 118
    during leave to care for a domestic partner, 61
    during pregnancy disability leave, 29
    during sick leave, 118

Paid time off (PTO)
    accrual of, 121, 124–125
    administration of, 122–124
    as a form of wages, 121
    as sick leave, 121, 122
    benefits during, 125
    eligibility for, 124, 125
    employee handbook on, 122, 123, 125
    employee reporting time off as, 125
    for kin care, 123
    forfeiture of, 124
    forms related to, 126
    interaction with workers' compensation, 123
    notice requirements for, 122
    paid family leave benefits during, 123
    pay during, 124–125
    pay for unused, 121, 124, 125
    poster requirements for, 122
    purposes of, 121
    request for, 122, 125
    requirement to provide, 121
    state disability insurance benefits during, 123
    using before accrual of, 123
    using during disability leave, 80
    using during family medical leave, 61–62, 122
    using during pregnancy disability leave, 28, 122
    using during sick leave, 123
    vs. vacation, 121, 122
    written notice of accrued amount, 123

Paid Time Off Policy, information on, 126

Parents of employees
    and bereavement leave, 162
    family medical leave to care for, 44
    kin care to care for, 115
    medical certification for, 50, 51, 117
    serious health condition of, 44

Part-time employees, family medical leave for, 46

PDL Checklist for Employer Compliance (5–49 Employees), information on, 38

PDL Documentation - For Employer Use Only (5–49 Employees), information on, 16, 23, 39

PDL. *See* Pregnancy disability leave

PDL/FMLA Checklist for Employer Compliance (50 or More Employees), information on, 16, 39, 42, 53

PDL/FMLA Documentation - For Employer Use Only (50 or More Employees), information on, 16, 23, 39, 42, 53

Personal holidays
    employee handbook on, 158
    forfeiture of, 157
    pay for unused, 157
    providing, 155

Personal leave of absence
    See also Sabbaticals
    benefits during, 163–164
    duration of, 163
    eligibility for, 162–163
    employee handbook on, 163–164
    pay during, 163
    reinstatement after, 163, 164

PFL. *See* Paid family leave (PFL) benefits

Physicians. *See* Health care providers

Posters
- for disability leave, 75
- for family medical leave, 47–48
- for military service leave, 127
- for paid family leave, 109
- for paid time off, 122
- for pregnancy disability leave, 18–19
- for sick leave, 116
- for state disability insurance, 104
- for vacation, 122
- for workers' compensation, 87

Pregnancy
- and termination of employee, 17
- and transfer of employee, 20, 21–22
- employees "disabled" by. *See* Pregnancy disability leave
- reasonable accommodation for, 23–26

Pregnancy disability leave (PDL)
- administration of, 23–27
- benefits during, 30–32
- denying request for, 20
- duration of, 16, 23–26
- eligibility for, 16
- employee handbook on, 19, 31
- employers who must provide, 17
- extended, 16, 25
- forms related to, 35–40
- interaction with baby bonding family leave, 25
- interaction with family medical leave, 3, 26
- interaction with workers' compensation, 29
- intermittent, 16, 22, 24
- layoff during, 34
- medical certification for, 20–21
- notice requirements for, 18–19
- paid family leave benefits during, 29
- pay during, 27–29
- poster requirements for, 18–19
- purposes of, 16
- qualifying events, 17–18
- reinstatement after, 32–35
  - refusal of, 33–34
  - to comparable position, 33
  - to different position, 33
  - to different work schedule, 33
- request for, 20–22

- summary of requirements for, 15–16
- termination of employee during, 17
- using paid time off during, 28, 122
- using sick leave during, 28
- using vacation during, 28, 122

Pregnancy Disability Leave Policy (5 or More Employees), information on, 19, 39

Pregnancy Disability Leave Poster, information on, 18, 22, 40, 76

Privacy, and medical certifications, 27, 50, 53

PTO. *See* Paid time off

Public policy defined, 17

R

Reasonable accommodation
- definition of, 74, 78
- disability leave as a form of, 76–77, 78–79
- employer obligation to provide, 74
- for employee returning from military service leave, 130–131
- for employee returning from pregnancy disability leave, 32
- for individuals with disabilities, 71
- interactive process for, 77
- job transfer as, 81
- medical certification of need for, 81
- modified schedule as, 81

Rehabilitation, alcohol or drug. *See* Alcohol rehabilitation; Drug rehabilitation

Reinstatement
- after disability leave, 81
  - guarantee of, 79
  - refusal of, 81
- after family medical leave, 64
  - guarantee of, 64
  - refusal of, 65–66, 66
  - to comparable position, 65
  - to different position, 65
- after kin care, 119
- after pregnancy disability leave, 32–35
  - refusal of, 33–34
  - to comparable position, 33
- after sick leave, 119

Release to return to work, 81, 116, 117

Request for Use of Kin Care, information on, 52, 105, 117, 120

S

Sabbaticals, 165
   See also Personal leave of absence

School activities leave
   See also School appearance leave
   administration of, 148
   benefits during, 147
   definition of, 146
   documentation for, 147
   duration of, 147
   eligibility for, 146–147
   forms related to, 152
   pay during, 147
   reinstatement after, 148

School Activities Policy, information on, 148, 152

School appearance leave
   See also School activities leave
   administration of, 146
   benefits during, 146
   definition of, 145
   documentation for, 145
   eligibility for, 145
   pay during, 145
   reinstatement after, 146

SDI. *See* State disability insurance (SDI) benefits

Serious health condition
   and medical certificates, 51
   definition of, 44–45

Sexual assault victim leave
   administration of, 137–138
   benefits during, 136
   definition of, 134
   documentation for, 135–136
   eligibility for, 135
   pay during, 136
   reinstatement after, 137

Sexual orientation, excluded as a disability, 73

Sick leave
   See also Kin care
   accrual of, 117, 119
   administration of, 117
   benefits during, 118–119
   definition of, 115
   employee handbook on, 117, 119
   employee reporting time off as, 119
   forfeiture of, 119
   forms related to, 120
   medical certification for, 116, 117
   notice requirements for, 116
   paid family leave benefits during, 118
   paid family leave during, 118
   paid time off as, 121, 122
   pay during, 117–118
   poster requirements for, 116
   purposes of, 115
   qualifying events, 116
   reinstatement after, 119
   request for, 116–117
   requirements to provide, 115
   requiring use of during unpaid leave, 116, 119
   state disability insurance benefits during, 118
   unpaid, 164
   using during disability leave, 80
   using during family medical leave, 61–62, 118
   using during paid time off, 123
   using during pregnancy disability leave, 28
   using during vacation, 123

Sick Leave Policy, information on, 116, 120

Spouses of employees
   and bereavement leave, 162
   family medical leave to care for, 44
   kin care to care for, 115
   medical certification for, 50, 51, 117
   serious health condition of, 44

State disability insurance (SDI) benefits
   and paid time off, 123
   and vacation, 123
   base period for, 118

coordinating with workers' compensation, 29
during disability leave, 79
during family medical leave, 60–62
during sick leave, 118

State Disability Insurance Provisions (DE 2515), information on, 22, 52, 76, 104, 113

Summary of Work-Related Injuries and Illnesses (Form 300A), information on, 91, 98

T

Temporary Transfers Policy, information on, 22, 40

Termination
during disability leave, 79, 81
during family medical leave, 51, 64, 66, 67
during pregnancy disability leave, 17

Time Off for Voting Policy, information on, 149, 152

Time Off for Voting, information on, 149

Training
See also Education leave
paying for optional, 166
paying for required, 166

Training time, pay during, 166

Transfer
as reasonable accommodation, 81
of employee on disability leave, 81
of pregnant employee, 20, 21–22

U

Undue hardship
and reinstatement rights, 79, 81
definition of, 74
determination of, 78–79

Uniformed Services Employment and Reemployment Rights Act of 1994 (USERRA), 7, 127, 131

Unpaid personal leave. *See* Personal leave of absence

Unpaid sick leave, 164

"Use it or lose it" policy
for floating holidays, 160
for vacation/paid time off, 125

USERRA. *See* Uniformed Services Employment and Reemployment Rights Act of 1994

V

Vacation
accrual during, 122
accrual of, 121, 124–125
administration of, 122–124
as a form of wages, 121
benefits during, 125
eligibility for, 124, 125
employee handbook on, 122, 123, 125
employee reporting time off as, 125
forfeiture of, 124
forms related to, 126
interaction with workers' compensation, 123
notice requirements for, 122
paid family leave benefits during, 123
pay during, 124–125
pay for unused, 121, 124, 125
poster requirements for, 122
purposes of, 121
request for, 122, 125
requirement to provide, 121
state disability insurance benefits during, 123
using before accrual of, 123
using during baby bonding family leave, 29
using during disability leave, 80
using during family medical leave, 61–62, 122
using during pregnancy disability leave, 28, 122
using during sick leave, 123
vs. paid time off, 121, 122
written notice of accrued amount, 123

Vacation Policy, information on, 126

Veterans Benefits Improvement Act of 2004 (VBIA), 127

Victims of crime leave
    administration of, 140–141
    benefits during, 140
    definition of, 138
    documentation for, 139
    eligibility for, 138–139
    forms related to, 152
    pay during, 139–140
    reinstatement after, 140

Victims of Crime Leave Policy, information on, 140, 152

Volunteer civil service leave
    administration of, 144
    benefits during, 144
    definition of, 143
    documentation for, 143
    eligibility for, 143
    forms related to, 153
    pay during, 143–144
    reinstatement after, 144

Volunteer Civil Service Personnel Policy, information on, 144, 153

Voting leave
    administration of, 149
    definition of, 148
    documentation for, 149
    duration of, 149
    forms related to, 152
    timing of, 149

W

Wage(s)
    claims for unpaid, 125, 160
    deductions from
        for absences due to illness, 115
        for advances of paid time off, 123
        for advances of vacation, 123
        for overpayment of sick leave, 117
    paid time off as a form of, 121, 124–125
    vacation as a form of, 121, 124–125

Witness duty leave
    administration of, 134
    benefits during, 133
    documentation for, 133
    eligibility for, 132
    forms related to, 152
    pay during, 133
    reinstatement after, 133–134

Workers' compensation
    coordinating with state disability insurance benefits, 29
    forms related to, 96–98
    interaction with disability leave, 4, 80
    interaction with family medical leave, 4
    interaction with pregnancy disability leave, 4, 29
    pamphlet on, 87
    using paid time off (PTO) during, 123
    using vacation during, 123

Workers' Compensation Policy, information on, 92, 98

Workweeks
    definition of, for family medical leave, 46
    definition of, for pregnancy disability leave, 23